444 DAYS

The American Hostage Story

444 DAYS
The American Hostage Story

by Sid Moody

and the News Staff and Photographers of
The Associated Press

Project Director: Dan Perkes
Editor: Norm Goldstein
Photo Editor: Grant Lamos

The Rutledge Press

New York, New York

Composition by Pulsar Graphics, Freehold, New Jersey
Printed and bound by Kingsport Press, Kingsport, Tennessee

Copyright © 1981 by The Associated Press

All rights reserved. No part of this book may be
reproduced or transmitted in any form or by any
means, electronic or mechanical, including photocopying,
recording or by any information retrieval system,
without permission in writing from the Publisher.

Published by The Rutledge Press

Distributed by W. H. Smith Publishers Inc., 575 Lexington Avenue,
New York, NY 10022.

First printing 1981.
Printed in the United States of America.

ISBN: cloth 0-8317-4570-3
       paper 0-8317-4571-1

CONTENTS

INTRODUCTION

Surely very few news events in our time kept so many Americans moved, engrossed, and enraged for so long as the protracted captivity of the small group of their compatriots in Iran.

Other matters might strike closer to home: The economy, the energy worries, the political campaigns and the election; but through it all was a nagging, persistent chord, the awareness of those hapless hostages in Tehran.

They were seized, with what premeditation nobody knows, in a theatrical burst of Iranian fury over the admission of their deposed Shah to the United States for medical treatment.

They would be held, said those anonymous but now famous "student militants" who seized them, until the Shah and his wealth were returned to the new Islamic Republic.

That was something clearly against the power and conscience of the United States to arrange. And the seizure of those American diplomats and aides at the U.S. Embassy was clearly in violation of international law and the long-established custom of civilized nations.

Hardly anyone at the time thought the drama would stretch to many months, into a second year. But the captivity wore on. The early televised demonstrations at the embassy gave way to factional infighting within the Iranian government, with the hostages as pawns. American outrage deepened.

But what could be done, short of wreaking military vengeance on the Ayatollah Khomeini's government—and thereby sacrificing the lives of the captives?

Economic sanctions were tried, and didn't have much effect. America's allies paid lip-service, and sometimes went beyond it, and that didn't help much, either.

Finally, in April 1980, a military rescue attempt was made—and floundered in a debris-strewn Iranian desert.

Some Americans blamed the president for trying, more blamed him for failing. Anger and frustration boiled up again in the country, as they had so often before during the impasse, and may have played a part in Jimmy Carter's defeat in November. Election Day fell on the first anniversary of the embassy seizure.

Meantime, the Shah died in July, after weary wanderings in his final refuge of Egypt. Many thought his disappearance from the scene would soften Iran's attitude.

But at Christmas, 1980, the hostages were still captive. The Iranians permitted them to send televised messages to their families and fellow Americans. They were well, they said. They were keeping their spirits up, they said. They hoped the monstrous separation wouldn't last much longer. They had said the same things on Christmas, 1979.

The families of the hostages carried on as best they could. For month after month, news of their loved ones was scant. The State Department and the press tried to keep the families informed, but neither press nor government could penetrate deeply into mysteries of Ayatollah Khomeini's government.

In Tehran, leaders issued statements and sent signals only to withdraw them a few days later or see them repudiated by other leaders. For a time, the United States despaired of negotiating with anyone.

With the approach of the national election, the momentum picked up again. Some Iranians, at least, preferred to try to reach a deal with Carter—a known quantity to them—rather than prolong the affair into a Reagan administration.

The end came in the final days of the Carter presidency. The long-deferred hour of freedom struck.

It may be years until the twists and turns of that long road are fully understood. Sid Moody's book however, pulls together all the available facts and presents the saga of the hostages as it unfolded and doubled back, took different tacks, raising and dashing hopes and keeping things in suspense until the very last.

He follows the story through days of hope and days of despair, in Tehran and Washington and elsewhere in the world. It makes a singularly absorbing chapter of American history.

Rene J. Cappon
General News Editor
The Associated Press

Day of rest or not, the Sunday paper thumped on the front porch that November 4, 1979, heavy with woe. Five killed, live, right on TV, at an anti-Klan rally in Greensboro, North Carolina. Assassinated President Park Chung-hee buried in South Korea. Mamie Eisenhower buried beside her husband in Abilene, Kansas. Jimmy Carter could look forward to a year of uphill toil. Ted Kennedy, who led him two-to-one in the polls, was about to throw his hat in the ring for the presidential election exactly one year away. The Shah of Iran was in Manhattan for cancer treatment, and a group had chained itself to the Statue of Liberty in protest. Back in Tehran it was raining and it was also...

DAY 1

Sunday in Tehran was just another day. Moslems observe their sabbath on Friday. This, however, did not keep the usual throngs from gathering in the street outside the beleagured United States Embassy. There wasn't all that much else to do. The country was all but paralyzed by economic and political chaos. What if oil production was down to a drip? If no one was quite in charge now that the Shah had fled his Peacock Throne? There was always time to clamor outside the embassy and shout "Death to Carter!" and burn an American flag. Better that than classes at Tehran University about a mile down the road from the twenty-seven acre embassy compound on Takht E-Jamshid Avenue.

For the one hundred or so employees inside the embassy, international diplomacy simply marked another day on the calendar, making do as best it could. The acting boss, Charge d'Affaires L. Bruce Laingen, had an appointment crosstown at the Foreign Ministry. He took two aides with him. Laingen had been in charge since April when Ambassador William Sullivan had returned to Washington. The fifty-six-year-old Sullivan was a career diplomat, outspoken and given to wielding a Big Stick. Or barbed tongue. As ambassador to Laos in the 1960s he was not above calling in air strikes against Viet Cong supply lines. Subsequently, as ambassador to the Philippines, he asked Imelda Marcos, the glamorous wife of President Ferdinand Marcos, why more had not been done to cure poverty in her country. "I don't know what else we could have done," she answered. "You could try feeding them cake," Sullivan countered, borrowing a phrase from Marie Antoinette.

Confronted with the uproar from the students, said one Washingtonian, "the old Bill Sullivan would be calling in air

strikes on the universities." But this was another time and another place, and Uncle Sam's Big Stick in Iran was a handful of Marines inside the embassy, a place whose residents mordantly called "Fort Apache."

One of the new boys in the compound was Air Force Lt. Col. David Roeder, a veteran of one hundred-plus missions in Vietnam. He had arrived just three days before in Tehran to settle in as deputy air attache. Rick Kupke, on the other hand, was due to go back to the States the next day. Kupke was completing a volunteer tour in the communications section.

Over in the consular section, Mark Lijek wasn't going anywhere. A short, smiling, light-haired man, he was doing his bit in the boiler room of international diplomacy, helping a fellow American with a problem. Kim King had lost his passport. Not only that, he had overstayed his visa, originally good for six months. King, a tourist from Oregon, had stayed on to help teach local businessmen English. Lijek was seeing what he could do when a woman down the hall cried: "They're coming over the wall!"

Well, that was somebodys else's problem. It wasn't the first time some nut had jumped the fence at Fort Apache.

     •   •   •

For several years Iran had been an explosion waiting to happen. It had all the ingredients where an uncontrolled cadence can lead to things like world wars. Oil, for instance, a most volatile substance in such times whether being pumped or not. Big power rivalry: the United States, losing its grip, and Russia, an historic imperialist in the area, long covetous of extending its own. A faltering despot who decreed reform but enforced it with a brutal secret police. A ruler who crowned himself with his own hands, as had Napoleon, King of Kings with a diadem of egret plumes and 3,755 jewels, yet was increasingly feared—and despised. An elderly religious of fiery visage who preached a faith that defied the West and its modern ways—and some would come to say, defied logic. Absent the oil and absent the Great Powers and Iran might have been a curiosity for historians. But Allah and geology had willed otherwise.

It was an ancient land, known to antiquity and since as Persia. In its modern epoch it had first been a pawn between Russia, which in the 19th century had been relentlessly extending its domain into Turkestan and Transcaspia, and Great Britain, intent on protecting its trade routes to India. The discovery of oil in 1908 by the British in the Zagros Mountains some 150 miles from the Persian Gulf added a new dimension to the competition. The resultant Anglo-Iranian Oil Company became a prominent factor in the af-

The flag burns. Iranian students at the U.S. Embassy. Why are the signs in English?

fairs of the poor, underdeveloped nation. As the Energy Age mushroomed, so did the strategic significance of Persia . The tribal, feudal patchwork of the country was ruled over by the kings of the Qajar dynasty, absolute monarchs as had been the custom in Persia for 2,000 years. Their authority rested on divine claims, but they were increasingly weak and corrupt. A brief Western-inspired reform led to a constitution in 1906 and formation of a parliament, the Majlis. But the dynasty lingered until 1921 when power was seized by Reza Khan, a onetime illiterate private who had risen to command of the Persian Cossack Brigade. With concurrence of the Majlis, he became Shah of Iran in 1925, taking the name Iran from the Ayran tribes who had first settled the country of whom the Persians were but one. Reza Shah adopted the name Pahlavi for his dynasty, taken from the language spoken by the ancient Parthians.

To insure an overland supply route during World War II, Britain occupied southern Iran and Russia the northern portion including Tehran. Reza Shah was not warm to the idea and was packed off to South Africa in 1941 to be succeeded by his twenty-two-year-old son, Mohammad Reza Pahlavi. The young, falcon-profiled monarch thought he was by birth qualified to rule. He startled his classmates once at their Swiss boarding school by entering the commons room and announcing: "When I enter a room, everyone rises."

With World War II over and Britain hemorrhaging, the United States began playing a greater role in Iranian affairs, a role that had been negligible. With U.S. support, the Shah sent troops to Azerbaijan in northwest Iran in 1946 to oust a puppet regime that had been left by the departing Russians. President Harry S. Truman stressed the importance Iran now held: "If the Russians were to control Iran's oil, either directly or indirectly, the raw material balance of the world would undergo serious damage, and it would be a serious loss for the economy of the Western World."

Thus was a marriage formed in petroleum.

The groom, however, seemed more intent on becoming the playboy of the Western world. He became a familiar figure in the Alps during skiing season. He craved speed—flying his own planes or driving his own racing cars. He was not indifferent to beauty, which kept gossip columnists titillated and family portraits photogenic. His father picked out his first wife before his son ever saw her. She was Princess Fawzia, sister of Egypt's King Farouk, a gluttonous jet setter. They were divorced in 1948 in favor of Princess Soraya who was in turn divorced ten years later, because she had borne no sons, in favor of Princess Farah. They had four children, two of them sons, so with the heredity assured, the father felt he could officially crown himself Shah, which he did on his

forty-eighth birthday. If his crown fit securely then, it had almost toppled several years earlier.

In the postwar period, the Majlis gained power while the Shah pleasured. In 1951, Prime Minister Mohammad Mossadegh nationalized the Anglo-Iranian Oil Company, which many of his countrymen, humiliated by the wartime occupation, thought was a good idea. Two years later Mossadegh was challenging the authority of the Shah himself. The street crowds caught fire, and the Shah hurriedly flew off to Europe, himself at the controls. Six days later, while shopping on Rome's Via Veneto, he heard that Mossadegh had been overthrown and that it was safe to come home which he did. The Central Intelligence Agency had in large part helped hand the Shah back his crown. Iran and the United States seemed destined to live happily ever after.

The Shah's dowry was, of course, oil. Uncle Sam brought to the marriage goodies that would delight the heart of any man who had declared himself King of Kings, Light of the Ayrans. Earth-shuddering tanks. Silvery Mach 2 jets that the Shah liked to test fly himself, swooping about over the plant at McDonnell Douglas while the adjacent St. Louis airport was closed to less imperious traffic.

As the sixties faded into the seventies and the hands

Mohammad Mossadegh. Fiery millionaire who brought about nationalization of the oil industry. He died in a village outside Tehran, an exile in his own land.

The Once and Future King. His first wife

A certain beauty. The Royal couple aboard the Queen Mary on a visit to England. ◬

King of Kings. At twenty-two, Mohammed Reza Shah Pahlavi became ruler of Iran when his father was exiled. Here, at twenty-seven in 1946, wearing his army's uniform, he poses in his study. ◬

14

The Crown of State. Egret plumes and 3,755 jewels. ◬

A Coronation. *The Shah places the crown on the head of Empress Farah, his third wife. She bore him sons.* △

He is forty. She is twenty-one. She wears a diamond tiara and a flowing bluish gray gown. By Dior. ▷

15

that owned the oil spiggots realized they might also control them, it served to make a rich Shah even richer. In 1971, to celebrate the 2,500th anniversary of the Persian monarchy, he threw a $100 million birthday party at Persepolis. One-hundred-sixty-five chefs were flown in from Paris. Courtiers sported Lanvin-designed uniforms stitched with a mile of gold thread each. Meanwhile the black gold poured from the ground at the rate of six million barrels daily, making Iran the world's second largest exporter of oil. When the Organization of Petroleum Exporting Countries (OPEC) embargoed oil after the Yom Kippur War in 1973, the Shah demurred. But he was in the forefront when OPEC began pumping up the price of oil. For the Shah had a dream. He would make his land of thirty-eight million people a world power. Or at least a regional one.

With American blessing, he poured oil revenues into the best, most sophisticated military hardware money could buy. Huge sums went into new factories, roads, high rise buildings, telecommunications. Twenty nuclear reactors were contracted for against the day the wells ran dry. By such time the Shah was determined that Iran would be able to stand tall in the world. It all had its price, however.

His series of economic plans tended to give more to things rather than people. While he had raised the literacy rate from five percent to forty percent during his reign, education had not been the highest priority in his spending. There were not enough trained people to operate all his new toys. So he brought in up to 70,000 Americans to help him do so. This did not sit well with some Iranian pride. His gleaming new cities drew off workers from the farms. Agricultural production faltered. Inflation ensued. Iran began bartering oil for food, a commodity in which she had once been self-sufficient. While he ordered twenty million acres redistributed to the poor, some of the land belonged to the Islamic mullahs, defenders of the faith and increasingly antagonists of the Shah. While city towers grew, many of the country's 66,000 villages still lacked running water. Envy grew between the oil-rich haves and the rural have nots.

The Shah outlawed the Communist Party, and in 1977 President Carter told him: "Iran is an island of stability in one of the most troubled areas of the world. This is a great tribute to you, Your Majesty, and to your leadership and to the respect, admiration and love which your people give to you."

16   *Bludgeons. They cannot stop what goes on in people's heads.* △   *Omens. Iranian troops and American Marines had to repel a Tehran mob on Christmas Eve, 1978.* ▷

It was a respect sometimes brutally enforced by the Shah's secret police, SAVAK.

The growing maladjustments of a force-fed society and economy had no outlet in a political process. The absolute ruler had decreed but one party with a token allowance for dissent. "The country lacked the necessary safety valves whereby its people, individually or collectively, could lawfully voice their grievances, demands or expectations," wrote Aimin Saikal in his book, *The Rise and Fall of the Shah.* "By 1977, a national tragedy had occurred: SAVAK had become so pervasive that a majority of Iranians could not even trust each other, let alone the government. They had become increasingly resentful of the Shah's system, with which they could not identify themselves." The public had become apathetic, but to give it voice the Shah feared would weaken his power.

There as a voice, however, that of Ayatollah Ruhollah Khomeini. He was a holy man, his title an honorific bestowed on him by his following. Ayatollah means "sign of God." Under that sign, Khomeini spoke from exile in a bungalow in Neauphle-le-Chateau outside Paris.

"Learn from the Prophet and be patient," said the Ayatollah. "He fought all his life to overcome oppression. And we have been doing it only a short time. But what are we afraid of? If we are killed, we will go to heaven. And if we

kill, we will go to heaven. This is the logic of Islam because we are in the right."

The Ayatollah's messages were secreted into Iran on cassette tapes and hawked in the bazaars for $1.25. They were a catalyst. Wrote Saikal: "In fact, a large number of people who followed Khomeini were not necessarily practicing Moslems. Nor did they agree with Khomeini's idea of an Islamic Republic. They followed him because they shared a common opposition to the Shah's rule. But because the Islamic message had a wide appeal to the Iranian masses, who had been imbued with it for centuries, Khomeini and his supporters were ultimately able to seize political power." But not without bloodshed.

"Nobody influences me, nobody!" the Shah once boasted. But by 1978 there was handwriting on the walls. It read:"Death to the Shah!" Strikes shut down the oil fields. Riots swept the cities. Khomeini's followers said 100,000 died, but others put the toll much lower. Protest, however, was now written in blood. An army colonel ordered his men to fire on a group of demonstrators in Tabriz shortly before Christmas. The mob beat the officer to death while the soldiers dropped their guns. The garrison was withdrawn from the city. The army, on which the Shah had lavished so much,was cracking. Shortly afterwards, in Tehran, a funeral procession made its way through the streets with the body of

18

a professor shot while encouraging demonstrators from the balcony of the Education Ministry. A company of the Shah's elite rangers accompanied them to preserve order. Some regular soldiers guarding Tehran University challenged the crowd. A colonel of the rangers stepped out waving his arms crying, "No, no, no!" The guards shot him down and the two military units began firing at each other.

The middle class began joining the youths of Tehran in harassing the uniformed soldiers in the street. Said one, an American-educated architect: "Until now, I have merely watched what has been going on. But now everything has gone too far. I felt I would be betraying my country by not joining these kids."

The Shah, at his moment of crisis, wavered. "You have to be an ornithologist to know what is going on in that peacock head," said one diplomat. On January 16, 1979, the Shah decided. He took flight for Egypt and a welcome from President Anwar Sadat. The Shah's aides said it was only a vacation.

But he would never again sit on the Peacock Throne.

·   ·   ·

"The holy one has come!" cried the multitudes as a tricolored Air France 747 squatted in for a landing at Tehran's Mehrabad Airport. Exit Shah, enter Khomeini. Throngs stretched to the horizon as the gray-cloaked Ayatollah slipped his way down the landing ladder. His eyes were piercing as an eagle's, but his flight had not been that certain. Khomeini's aides agreed to fly the jumbo jet half full so it would have enough fuel to return to France if landing permission were denied in Tehran.

There was little chance of that. The mob, armed to the eyebrows, owned the capital, and the Ayatollah owned the mob. The Shah's vaunted army had melted away, dissuaded by the United States from any last moment heroics and helplessly divided within itself as well. Mosques were now armories, and every conceivable gun was being carried by every conceivable person. When a mullah tried to disarm one youth, he was shot to death.

Khomeini wasted little time. "We are only victorious when we can cut the hands of the foreigners from our lands," he told his clamoring followers at the airport. Millions lined the road as he drove to Behesht-Zahra cemetery where many SAVAK victims and other fallen were buried. Then he proceeded into the city to set up his revolution's headquarters in the Alavi elementary school, located among the bazaars.

Clearly interpreting the Ayatollah's intentions, the United States hurriedly began flying out Americans in chartered Pan American 747s. Military transports and helicopters were standing by in Turkey if needed. But the Iranians

An old friendship. The Shah said it was a vacation when he visited Anwar Sadat in Egypt in 1979. He never returned home.

After a fourteen-year exile, the Ayatollah returns to Tehran. He will be heard. It is February, 1979.

let them go in relative peace. The only Americans left were the reporters and camera crews and the one hundred or so in Fort Apache.

. . .

The Shah had left the government in the hands of the Prime Minister Shahpour Bakhtiar, hands that were handcuffed by the anarchy of Tehran's streets. Khomeini swiftly removed him, saying any Shah appointment was illegal. He eventually would be replaced by a veteran politician, Mehdi Bazargan who told reporters fruitful relations with the U.S. are "most definitely possible." As if to emphasize this sign of good will, the Ayatollah called for his followers to turn in their weapons. The date was February 13, the day before St. Valentine's Day.

Armed mobs outside the U.S. Embassy were nothing new. In December an Iranian policeman was fatally wounded in a scuffle at the gates. Shortly thereafter, the nineteen-Marine garrison broke up another demonstration with tear gas. They were obviously outgunned, but no reinforcements had been sent. Washington was waiting and seeing. Just after ten A.M. on February 14, the waiting stopped abruptly. Demonstrators on rooftops opened up on the embassy with a barrage of small arms and machine gun fire. The nineteen Marines hastily donned helmets and flak jackets and began laying down a cloud of tear gas. Sullivan and the defense attache, Col. Leland Holland, set up a command post in the ambassador's second floor office. Sullivan's code name over the walkie-talkies was "Cowboy."

"Cowboy, should the Marines use their shotguns as well?" "No," Sullivan replied. On further thought: "If you need to protect yourself, you may fire. If you can arrange to surrender, do so."

If it was an order, it was also a precedent. During the airlift, the embassy had said, "We cannot protect American lives in Iran." Now it was evident it could not, or would not, protect them inside Fort Apache, American territory under international law.

The Iranian attackers smashed down the embassy gates. The Americans fled to the windowless communications room on the second floor of the chancery. Burn bags were stuffed into incinerators. A radio operator smashed $500,000 worth of equipment and coding gear with a sledgehammer.

The attackers ran through the tear gas and set up the staircase. "Everybody get down," commanded an Iranian in a camouflage jacket and blue work pants.

"I was never scared during the assault from the outside because we knew the bullets would never penetrate the walls," said Ken Freed of the *Los Angeles Times* who had never been in the embassy. "But I really got scared five minutes before the finish. We could hear tremendous shooting and arguing downstairs and then a long burst of automatic fire. I thought we were going to die for sure."

Attackers ran through the building herding Americans. Some stopped to dial telephones. One shouted to whomever answered: "Hey Yankee, we've come to do you in. Tell Carter he's finished."

The Americans were led in groups from the building, Sullivan among them at bayonet point. Some bystanders tried to punch an American in the head. His guard shooed them off by firing into the air. A woman from the embassy swung her fists in the air to warn off any attackers. There were cooler heads among the Iranians. At the university, where Khomeini loyalists were turning in their guns, two men rushed in to spread the news. "The U.S. Embassy is under attack. Let's go stop it!" A group rushed off in a jeep to the scene.

Deputy Prime Minister Ibrahim Yazdi had also rushed to the embassy in a blue Mercedes. An air force colonel was trying to shout into a nonfunctioning bullhorn: "Don't shoot. Orders from Khomeini. This shooting is a conspiracy against Khomeini. For the honor of the country, please stop!"

"This is bad propaganda for the government," said a bystander. Finally order was restored, and the tear gas wafted off in the morning air. Two militia men had been killed as was an Iranian waiter from the embassy's Caravansary restaurant. Two Marines were slightly wounded.

. . .

The State Department was to identify the attackers as members of the left wing People's Sacrifice Guerrillas. But they were not the only ones shooting in Tehran.

Black clad women waving knives and meat cleavers milled outside Khomeini's frowzy schoolhouse headquarters. "We want to kill! Bring out the murderers!" They cried. Inside four of the Shah's generals were lead up to the roof by Khomeini gunmen. One of them was Gen. Nematollah Nassiri, former head of SAVAK. The four were blindfolded, bound and then shot in the back of the head. One of the militiamen descended to the crowd outside.

"You can go now," he said. "They have been killed."

Khomeini himself had ordered the executions after a drumhead trial. "They are the corrupt of the earth," the holy man said. "This was done to purify the blood of the revolution and to put new blood of the revolution into circulation."

In Tabriz, Khomeini's followers fought against Marxist guerrillas of a group calling themselves the People's Feday-

New names. Mehdi Bazargan is a key aide to the Ayatollah. He demands that the Shah-installed Bakhtiar government resign.

MEHDI BAZARGAN

The Ayatollah Khomeini proclaimed seventy-year-old Mehdi Bazargan head of the provisional government of Iran in February 1979. A soft-spoken former professor, engineer, human rights campaigner, and author of several books on modern civilization and Islam, Bazargan has a reputation in Iranian politics as a skillful troubleshooter. He attracted attention the previous year as head of the unofficial Iranian Human Rights Committee, exposing alleged rights violations by the agents of Shah Mohammad Reza Pahlavi's government.

Bazargan—described by one local Tehran newspaper as "so clean that no adjective can describe him"—is a veteran of anti-Shah campaigns and is viewed as a devout Moslem by the nation's religious activists. Western diplomats, who had feared a more radical choice as prime minister, considered him moderate on most political questions and believed he would lend a professional tone to Khomeini's government if it ever came to power.

Bazargan comes from the same political background as the provisional government's chief opponent, Prime Minister Shahpour Bakhtiar. Both men served in the 1951-53 socialist government of Mohammad Mossadegh, which briefly forced the Shah into exile before being overthrown itself in a military coup. Bakhtiar was undersecretary of labor and Bazargan headed the national oil industry.

Bazargan and Bakhtiar both went into opposition politics after Mossadegh's defeat and were jailed for their activities. But, while Bakhtiar changed camps and accepted the Shah's invitation to become prime minister, Bazargan remained in the Khomeini camp.

Early in 1979, as Khomeini's special envoy, Bazargan was the key figure in getting striking oil workers to agree to produce enough petroleum for domestic needs. He toured oilfields and lectured at mosques and political rallies, carrying Khomeini's orders to the oilmen and negotiating with the government's oil monopoly.

Bazargan earned a thermodynamics degree at the University of Paris at a time when study abroad was a rare thing for a young Iranian. He returned to his homeland in 1942 and taught at Tehran University. He won a reputation as one of Iran's best mathematicians and was awarded the chair of thermodynamics at the university's Technical College.

After World War II, he became increasingly involved in politics and was a close ally of Mossadegh, when he came to power. The leftist general stripped the British-owned Anglo-Iranian Oil Company of its assets in Iran's oil-rich Khuzestan Province and sent Barzagan to head oil operations there.

An anecdote from that period purports to show Bazargan's abhorrence of alcohol. He supposedly was told by associates that there was no further use for hundreds of cases of beer left behind by British oil workers in Khuzestan. Asked whether the state oil firm should sell the beer, Bazargan said, "We are here to sell oil and not beer. Dump the cases into the Shatt (an estuary off the Persian Gulf)."

After Mossadegh's ouster, Bazargan formed the opposition Liberation Movement with the participation of Moslem religious leader Ayatollah Mahmoud Taleghani of Tehran. The Liberation Movement and Bakhtiar's Iran Party were both affiliated with the National Front, the umbrella opposition group closely allied with Khomeini.

For his political activities, Bazargan was jailed, including one five-year term beginning in 1962, and sent into exile. In the late 1960s, he was barred from teaching. In 1978, he was arrested and kept in custody for ten days by the military government that preceded Bakhtiar in power.

een, and as many as 900 may have died. Khomeini irregulars or just the exuberant careened through Tehran shooting at hotels, police stations and radio stations. They took free rein as the army, resigned, ordered its men to remain in their barracks. A leading general had called the Shah in Morocco where he had gone from Egypt. It was reportedly a request for permission to stage a coup. The Shah refused to take the call.

And so the armories were opened to any takers. Ragtag youths in jeans took over the Shah's sumptuous Niavaran Palace as his Imperial Guards stood by, weeping. SAVAK headquarters was ransacked, its files strewn in the streets, its torture devices photographed, then burned. A pro-Shah general was shot by his own driver.

At the same time, in neighboring Afghanistan, the U.S. ambassador, Adolph Dubs, a fifty-eight year-old career diplomat, was abducted by three gunmen in Kabul. He and they died in an ensuing shootout.

In Iran, trying to make the best of a bad situation, the Carter Administration recognized Khomeini. "The only way we could have dealt with this problem differently was to have intervened massively," said one Carter official. "But how do you intervene massively in a country of 38 million people? We've done what we could to give external security and psychological and political support for the re-establishment of authority. We're watching an earthquake, and there's nothing we can do about it."

Said Sen. Howard Baker of Tennessee, still a candidate for the Republican presidential nomination: "There's a growing feeling that America is an international patsy."

•   •   •

In the following months, the newly rebuilt consular section where Mark Lijek was working on that Sunday morning in November was representative of what had been going on between Tehran and Washington: An Arabian Nights nightmare. One day there would be mobs in the street shouting death to just about whoever came to mind. The next day the consulate was besieged by Iranians trying to get visas to the United States.

Khomeini had gotten the oil field workers back to work, and the National Iranian Oil Company was selling 700,000 barrels a day to the United States, about 3.7 percent of her consumption. It had been 900,000 barrels daily when the Shah was on the Peacock Throne. On the other hand, the Ayatollah, who had taken up residence in the holy city of

Leftovers. Former President Nixon visits the exiled Shah, his wife, and his son on a rented estate in Cuernavaca, Mexico, in 1979. The son bears the name Reza.

23

So many voices. Former Iranian Prime Minister Shahpur Bakhtiar says the hostages could be released before the American election in 1980. He adds it will not affect the election.

SHAHPUR BAKHTIAR

Shahpur Bakhtiar, a slim, soft-spoken man with courtly manners, was once described as "a great diplomat: he can talk a lot without saying a damned thing." Those who know him best say his elegant manner masks a core of iron.

Born in Tehran, Bakhtiar attended high school in Beirut, Lebanon, and then studied political science and law at the Sorbonne in Paris. During World War II, he fought with the Free French. He is married to a French woman. When he returned to Iran in 1946, he could scarcely speak Persian. Several years later, a political opponent joked: "He goes to Paris for a haircut."

Bakhtiar served as deputy labor minister in the National Front, the 1951-53 government of Mohammad Mossadegh which almost succeeded in driving the Shah from power. While rising to the Number Two position in the National Front, he became a successful international lawyer. He was commonly regarded as a staunch anti-Communist and a politician untainted by corruption.

After serving under Mossadegh, Bakhtiar became the leader of the Bakhtiar Clan. In this capacity he commanded the loyalty of the nation's oldest and largest tribes, whose members in areas along Iran's southern flank formed about sixty percent of the work force in some oil fields.

Bakhtiar's cousin, Soraya, was empress until the Shah divorced her in 1958 because she had not borne a son. Teymour, another cousin, was appointed first commander of SAVAK, the Shah's secret police. However, Bakhtiar himself refused to join the Shah's government. In fact, he was imprisoned six times for anti-Shah activities. "I chose unemployment and prison rather than compromise my principles," he once said.

However, in an effort to avert the Islamic revolution, the late Shah appointed Bakhtiar prime minister in January 1979. When he accepted the position, he was expelled from the National Front for "betrayal." Bakhtiar served as prime minister for only thirty-nine days before going underground when Khomeini returned to Iran from exile in France. Several months later, he surfaced in Paris and announced he had begun to lead a resistance movement seeking to overthrow Khomeini's regime.

In April 1980, Bakhtiar was quoted as speculating that Soviet-trained Communists, backing Ayatollah Ruhollah Khomeini, would seize power when Khomeini dies. "They have money and they get precise instructions. When Khomeini dies, he will be replaced by these men," Bakhtiar warned. "And the day will come when they make an appeal for Soviet, East German and Czech technicians."

Bakhtiar's Western attitudes annoyed many Iranians, who despised similar traits in the Shah. In July 1980, he narrowly escaped an assassination attempt when Islamic extremists tried to shoot their way into his Paris apartment. A neighbor and a policemen were killed, and three other policemen were wounded. Bakhtiar was unharmed.

Late in 1980, Bakhtiar's support in Iran appeared to be slipping. He revealed that he had visited Iraq five times during 1980 and had been in Baghdad shortly before the border war between Iran and Iraq broke out.

Impromptu prison. The Foreign Ministry in Tehran where three American diplomats were held. ▷

Qum, was describing Washington, Carter and the United States in general as "the great Satan." Friendship with such a nation, he said, was as that of a wolf and a lamb. To make things even more absolutely unclear, Ibrahim Yazdi, now foreign minister, described ties between the two countries as "lukewarm but improving." As if to demonstrate this, Bazargan had chatted pleasantly for ninety minutes with U.S. National Security Adviser Zbigniew Brzezinski at a diplomatic function in Algiers.

That was on Thursday, November 1, 1979.

.   .   .

Whatever the state of relations between Iran and Washington, it was clear the state of the Shah's health was deteriorating. He had moved from Morocco to a villa in Cuernavaca, outside Mexico City. Washington had dissuaded him from seeking sanctuary in the United States. It said it could not insure his safety from the thousands of Iranian students in the country. Furthermore, it feared retaliation by Khomeini—an oil embargo or even violence to the handful of Americans still in Iran. Former Secretary of State Henry Kissinger and New York banker David Rockefeller reportedly argued the Shah's case, but the Carter administration said no. However, as the Shah's condition worsened, the President relented half way. The Shah could come to New York for treatment.

The embassy in Tehran said this would be a mistake in the face of clear threats from Khomeini's people. David Newsom, under-secretary of state for political affairs, concurred. He tried to talk Secretary of State Cyrus Vance into denying the Shah even temporary residence. Vance overruled him and advised Carter to go ahead. In late October, the Shah moved into a suite at New York Hospital under tight security. Iranian students in the United States promptly staged demonstrations. Washington reassured Tehran that the Shah was only allowed in on humanitarian grounds and would be leaving after examination and surgical treatment. Bazargan's government in turn twice told Washington it would protect Americans from any reaction. At the same time, Khomeini was saying that the American Embassy was "a nest of spies." At the embassy itself that Sunday morning, the usual crowd had gathered.

"Give us the Shah!" they shouted.

.   .   .

At 3:03 A.M. Washington time that morning, a commercial telephone rang in the seventh floor operations at the State Department. The senior watch officer, Robert S. Steven, answered it. It was an embassy officer calling from Tehran. Demonstrators had once again invaded the compound. "They do not appear to be violent," he added.

The mob had been milling around the embassy gate when a youth stepped forward with bolt cutters and cut the chain. There was a surge forward. The leaders seemed to

know where they were going. One said they had studied plans of the compound in advance. They had passes to show their own guards at the gates.

The Marines again fired tear gas, but nothing more. Someone phoned Laingen at the Foreign Ministry to notify him. Others called government offices asking for help. Battle hardened by now, embassy personnel hurried to the chancery, now protected with new steel grillwork and doors. Once again burn bags were put to the fire.

Attackers outside hollered through bullhorns: "Give up and you won't be harmed! If you don't give up, you will be killed!"

Shortly after noon, Laingen phoned to order "final destruction" of documents and equipment. This time there was no gunfire around the chancery. "If the Marines don't shoot, we take over," said one of the attackers. "If they do, we have our martyr. Either way we win."

The Marines' orders were to hold any assault at bay only long enough to permit the documents to be destroyed. Finally the Marine guard at the chancery door opened it. Students poured in, their eyes streaming from tear gas. They took the gas masks from embassy personnel inside. "We had the gas for three hours," said one. "Now you can taste it for a while." Then the Americans were blindfolded and ushered outside.

The attackers, calling themselves the Muslim Students of the Imam Khomeini Line, issued "Communique No. 1." It said they had seized the embassy because of "the U.S. offer of asylum to the criminal Shah who was responsible for the deaths of thousands of Iranians."

It had taken three hours for the group to take over the compound. This time the militia did not show up. The embassy had maintained telephone contact with Washington until 4:57 A.M., capital time, when a staff member told Steven: "Some of our people are being led out of here one by one." Then the phone went dead. When Steven called back, he got a busy signal.

When the woman in the consular building had said people were coming over the wall, Kim King went to the window for a look. There was no shooting. He concluded they must be police. An Iranian tried to break in through a window in the men's room. A Marine pushed him out and fired tear gas. Then the lights went out. "We realized then that we had to get out," King said later.

He and Lijek, Kathy Stafford, aged twenty-eight, a consular secretary from Crossville, Tennessee, and Robert Anders, aged fifty-four, a consulate officer from Port Charlotte, Florida, made for the rear of the building. A Marine pried open a back door that opened onto an alley. They scurried out as nonchalantly as possible from Fort Apache.

Power and glory. Iranian militants roughhouse the American flag.

27

2

Ronald Reagan formally announced his candidacy for President. George Meany, aged eighty-five, said farewell as head of the AFL-CIO. Phil Simms, a rookie, took over as quarterback for the N.Y. football Giants. Oliva Dionne, father of the famed quintuplets, died at age seventy-six, in Ontario. And it was . . .

DAY 9

President Carter was resting at Camp David in preparation for a two-day trip to Canada when he was notified that Sunday morning. He talked by phone throughout the day with Vance and Brzezinski. He arrived back at the White House at 8:15, his face set. He had promised a statement to the press but reconsidered. Khomeini's mob for the moment held the cards. They seized the British Embassy in Tehran for several hours that Monday before vacating it. The following day Prime Minister Bazargan and his Cabinet resigned. "I was always the last to know what was going on," Bazargan said in a final talk to the nation. "I found myself at a dead end." He also found himself contending with an emotional outburst against which statecraft was useless.

"You are weak, sir," the Ayatollah had told him. Khomeini's fifteen-man Revolutionary Council became the government. The Ayatollah's inflammatory and contradictory statements from Qum became the law in the land.

Notified of Bazargan's departure early in the morning, the President woke his principal aides, Hamilton Jordan and Jody Powell, and called them to a meeting with top-level strategists including Defense Secretary Harold Brown and the Joint Chiefs of Staff. Send in the Marines? The Airborne?

It was swiftly decided to refrain. The mob owned the streets of Tehran through which any force would have to fight. Although it was presumed, it was not known if the sixty-five or so hostages were still in the embassy. It was possible that their captors would kill them before they could be rescued. The one thing Jimmy Carter had decided, then and thereafter, was to save the hostages' lives.

Don't rock the boat, he pleaded with Congressional leaders at a breakfast meeting. "Don't call them murderers or torturers." The carrier Midway, with seven escort vessels was 2,500 miles from Iran in the Indian Ocean—it was the nearest sizeable American force. He ordered the task force to sail towards the Persian Gulf.

In this initial attempt at diplomacy, Carter called on former Attorney General Ramsey Clark to go to Tehran. Clark had spoken favorably of Khomeini and had visited the Ayatollah in France in January. Chosen to accompany Clark was William Miller, a former diplomat in Iran who spoke the language.

Clark and Miller reached Turkey but got no further after the Ayatollah declared: "Do they think the Spirit of God (himself) will converse with such evil characters?"

Meanwhile at the United Nations, just down the street from the Shah's hospital, the Security Council called for the hostages' release "without delay." The diplomats were not unmindful of a precedent that could make anyone's embassy fair game. Sadat, visibly angered, was even more outspoken. The seizure, he said, was "a disgrace to Islam."

•   •   •

The reaction of the American people, already fed an evening diet of burning U.S. flags and chants of death threats to their "satanic" selves on television news, was immediate and intense. In Los Angeles, onlookers took out their frustration on Iranian students demonstrating against the Shah with fists and any missiles at hand. Longshoremen refused to handle Iranian shipping. Mechanics would not service Iran Air planes. Americans across the country marched with signs and shouts inviting the 55,000 or so Iranian students—no one was certain how many there actually were—to pick up their books and go home. On November 10 Carter ordered immigration authorities to investigate how many of the students were in the United States illegally and to undertake deportation proceedings against them.

The focus of much of the uproar meanwhile lay in his $900-a-day hospital suite, his shrunken body looking "like a jockey's." He volunteered to leave the United States but the offer was turned down by Washington. The United States did not pay extortion, in coin or in persons. Besides, said an administration aide, "We can't move him. They've cut him open. He's got tubes hanging out of his body."

He was battling lymphatic cancer with complications, an ailment he had had for six years. He passed his time watching Westerns and reruns and welcoming such visitors as Kissinger and Richard Nixon. Demonstrators in the street outside carried placards calling for his death.

While Washington considered its options, Muhammad Ali offered himself in exchange for the hostages. "I'm a Muslim, and I'm known and loved in Iran," said the boxing ex-champ. There were no takers.

The Pentagon studied contingencies. A mockup of the embassy compound was reportedly built in the South, and jet pilots rehearsed hemstitching the sidewalks in strafing

Before his return. The Ayatollah, in exile, meets with former U.S. Attorney General Ramsey Clark, a would-be conciliator.

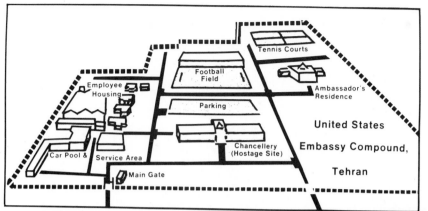

Stone walls do a prison make.
A layout of the American Embassy, Tehran.
The hostages were initially kept in the chancellery.

Day Two. Iranians pray outside the embassy for the students on hostage duty inside. They demand the Shah be deported from the United States.

Brief glimpses. All that Americans saw of their hostage countrymen, herded from place to place on the embassy grounds.

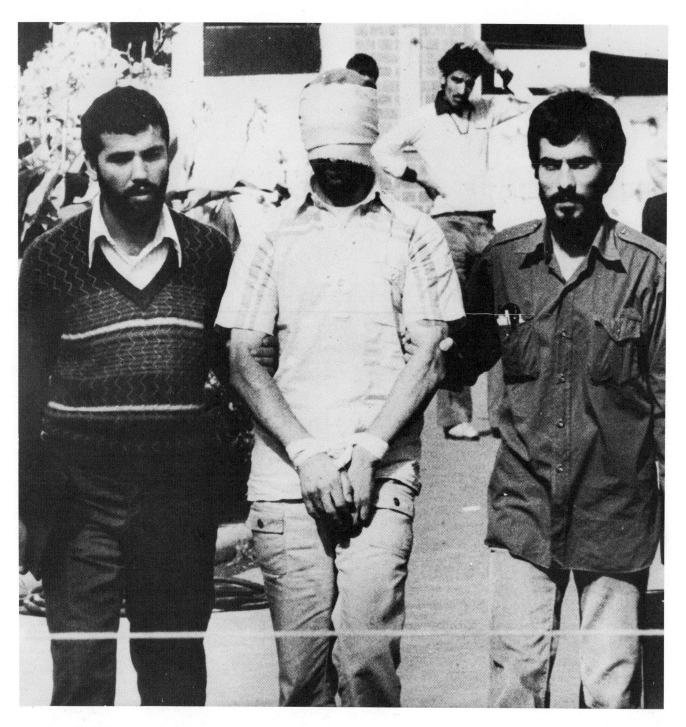

Day Three. Blindfolds become a symbol for humiliation.

runs. Two pilots were said to have crashed to their deaths during practice.

Frustration was the prevalent national mood. "We have reviewed our assets and our options, and they are precious few," said a Washington official. "Whom do you talk to? Whom do you deal with?" asked another. It's a situation of great instability. You don't know what's going to happen from one moment to the next."

To some the Ayatollah was engaged in a risky game, rallying the emotions of the Iranians around the hostage issue to stave off upheaval from the Communists and other leftist groups. By this scenario, the Americans were to be considered pawns, both in Iran and in the United States.

America did not lack for second guessers. Democratic Sen. Henry Jackson of Washington said "restraint is the order of the day." But newly-announced presidential candidate Ted Kennedy criticized the Carter Administration for unpreparedness. Students of Iranian history faulted the Carter Administration for minimizing the bitter animosity towards to Shah by both pro-Shah and pro-Khomeini Iranians.

As if in support, the captors made public documents they said they had found in the embassy. One, purporting to be a message from Vance to Laingen in July asked what Iranian reaction would be if the Shah were allowed to settle in

Anachronisms. A girl in a shawl on hostage duty. A walkie-talkie.

"Intelligence Nest." The Iranian students display electronic gear to support their contention that the embassy was a nest of spies.

34

Old Glory.

Taking out the garbage. The ultimate insult. △

Cartoons. Demonstrators carry a large painting depicting American puppeteering. Note that the caption is in English. ▷

◁ *The walls are the message. A girl gets a boost to put yet another poster on the embassy bricks.*

Fervent. Iranian women chant outside the embassy.

the United States in return for giving up his throne. "We understand the key to minimizing the impact of the Shah's admission would be . . . the government's willingness and ability in such a situation to control and command the security forces guarding our people . . ."

The captors paraded other documents that they said proved some of the hostages were CIA agents and threatened to try them as spies. The militants said that if the United States tried to rescue them, they would be put to death.

Reason having failed, on November 12, Carter stopped the importation of Iranian oil which represented about three percent of the U.S. supply. Iran struck at the pocketbook two days later, threatening to withdraw its deposits in U.S.

banks. It put the total at $12 billion. Carter was quicker. The same day he froze all Iranian assets in the United States. Bankers estimated this amounted to between $6 billion and $8 billion.

John Connally, another Republican still in the presidential race, said: "If appeasement were an art form, this administration would be the Rembrandt of our time."

But Jimmy Carter had struck back where he could. Whatever the amount the Iranians had in the bank, the United States at least had a bargaining chip.

On guard. An Iranian student in the embassy compound. Ten days after the takeover, the Iranian government says some hostages will be released "very soon." ▽

Fight back...
Drive 55!

A BILLBOARD EDITORIAL

ELLER

A Gallup poll showed President Carter's public approval had doubled overnight, the swiftest jump that organization had ever recorded. The Harris poll put him only four points behind Ted Kennedy. Newsweek's poll showed thirteen percent of Americans favoring return of the Shah to eighty-three percent opposed, sixty-seven percent were against a military rescue and it was . . .

DAY 16

By now the streets outside Fort Apache turned on and off with the stage violence of a professional wrestling bout. On camera, the mob gritted teeth, burned flags and cried "Death to Carter!"

"They only shout now when they see a sound camera," said an English newsman. Hawkers pushed through the crowd selling Coca-Cola. One was pushing boiled eggs. "Death to Carter!" he intoned. Then: "Eat boiled eggs." The crowd laughed and obligingly translated for American journalists. Others saluted American reporters with what little English they knew: "Welcome."

If the streets were quixotic, the government was even more so. Abbott and Costello would have given new life to their "Who's on first" routine trying to describe the Tower of Babble that conflicting government "spokesmen" had become.

Abolhassan Bani-Sadr, forty-seven-year-old acting foreign minister, is out. Sadegh Ghotbzadeh is in. Ghotbzadeh, aged forty-five, had been director of National Radio and Television. Bani-Sadr is now finance minister.

Bani-Sadr says the hostages can't be held indefinitely. Ghotbzadeh says they will be held until the Shah is returned. Before leaving the Foreign Ministry, Bani-Sadr says: "If the U.S. government intervenes militarily, all Iranians will fight to the last drop of blood." In almost the next breath he says: "The United States, as a land of free people, can neither submit to the humiliation of surrendering a sick man to a regime such as the Islamic Republic of Iran, nor can it take any pleasure in the humiliation of saving the lives of about 50 or 60 of its citizens by turning over this sick man."

Ghotbzadeh says: "Those who can be proved not to have consciously engaged in espionage will be freed." Would those convicted be killed? "I hope we don't reach that point. But on the face of earth, anything is possible." Chief Islamic prosecutor Hassan Ghafarpour doesn't hedge. Spies will be executed by firing squad. The militants inside the embassy

don't see eye to eye with Ghotbzadeh. "We will release nobody, nobody at all." To that, Ghotbzadeh says: "I continue to be caught between the students, the Revolutionary Council and the Imam (Khomeini). When there are restraints put on the students they become suspicious and we have to be careful. We cannot wound them or hurt their feelings. They listen only to the Imam, and nobody in the country can tell them anything."

That turns out to be less than accurate. In Tabriz, city of a million people in Azerbaijan in northwest Iran, mobs suddenly are heard shouting "Death to Khomeini!" They overpower some Khomeini supporters, shoot at others, and briefly hold their captives hostage. Their imam is also an ayatollah, Kazem Sharietmadari, a moderate and rival of Khomeini. The Azerbaijanis, like the Turkomans and Baluchis, are desirous of regional autonomy. The Kurds would rather be independent.

In one of the rare moments of unanimity, the Security Council of the United Nations voted fifteen-to-none calling for Iran to release the hostages "without delay." Even the Soviet Union votes "da." Iran boycotts the session in New York. Bani-Sadr, not surprisingly, says he would have gone if he were still foreign minister. But he isn't. Ghotbzadeh now is. He says the resolution is immaterial because it did not deal with the return of the Shah. On the other hand, he says, the resolution was "a step forward." Bani-Sadr says Iran, by boycotting, missed a chance to present its case against the Shah and American domination of his country to a world forum.

Then, on November 19, the militants, who say they are not going to release anybody, let three hostages free—two black Marines and a woman secretary. The next day they free ten more women and blacks. The move is obviously a move to win sympathy among racial and feminist groups in the United States. It doesn't.

The liberated thirteen, eight blacks and five women in all, were quickly flown to a U.S. military base in Germany and then home in time for Thanksgiving. They said little, but did for the first time give some indication what had been going on behind the walls of Fort Apache.

•   •   •

With the thirteen freed hostages accounted for, it was still not certain how many remained in Iranian hands. The Washington government never did publish a list. The number given most frequently at first was fifty. But sometimes it would be forty-nine. Laingen and his two aides were still interred at the Foreign Ministry, thus under control of the government. That much was known. Laingen sometimes could have access to the telephone and be somewhat cur-

Who speaks for Iran? Sadegh Ghotbzadeh replaces Bani-Sadr as foreign minister. Another new name for American television commentators. △

Who speaks for Iran? Abolhassan Bani-Sadr is forced out as foreign minister, then is elected president, but has no power. △

The lucky thirteen. The first hostages freed. Eight blacks and five women. Home for Thanksgiving, 1979. ▷

Appetizers. They released thirteen and kept the rest. △

rent. Those at the embassy were denied any contacts except with their captors.

They were not forgotten, whether or not they knew it. Vance had greeted the homecoming thirteen at Andrews Air Force Base outside Washington along with one hundred of their families. "Our relief that you are safe is muted by our concern for those who remain," he said. "The last hostage is just as important to us as the first."

Before they left Fort Apache, the liberated prisoners were questioned inside the compound in a public show by the militants. Why had counterfeit dollars, deutsche marks and Iranian rials been found inside the embassy? Wasn't this proof that the United States was trying to sabotage the Iranian economy?

"Oh, heavens, we weren't involved," said Joan Walsh, a secretary.

The militants also produced a forged Belgian passport made out in the name of Paul Timmermans and bearing the photograph of Thomas Ahern Jr., of Falls Church, Virginia. Ah-ha! CIA. Actually he was the embassy's narcotics control officer, a position of some confidentiality in a land where opium poppies were priced even higher than oil.

Ahern grew up in Fond du Lac, Wisconsin, son of a plumbing contractor. He was an Eagle Scout, basketball player and also adept at piano. He had served three years in the Army before joining the foreign service. Married and the father of a twelve-year-old daughter, he had come to Tehran that year.

"Very vibrant, an excellent student, fun loving in a quiet kind of way, also kind of introspective," a onetime classmate recalled.

Fond du Lac? Notre Dame?

A spy?

Like Ahern, the hostages were a composite of many things in American life. They came from all sections, were of various ages, served their country in many ways. Some were in the embassy on November 4 by sheerest coincidence, some because that's where their careers had taken them.

Jerry Plotkin was like the unwitting customer who walks in in the middle of a bank holdup. He had sold household goods out of Sherman Oaks, California. He had left his wife behind to come to Iran to see what fruits Khomeini's revolution might bear for some good old American enterprise. Unfortunately, he dropped by the embassy that Sunday morning, and that was that. Jerry Plotkin, aged forty-seven, became a hostage.

Bill Keough hadn't meant to be there either. Keough, aged forty-nine, from Waltham, Massachusetts, was on his way through to Pakistan. He was an educator and had been principal of the 4,000-student American School before it closed down following the Shah's departure.

He settled his six-foot-six-inch, 300-pound self temporarily near Washington, then was named principal of the International School in Islamabad. He arrived in Tehran November 1, on his way to his new post, to pick up some papers. The embassy put him up for his short stay. It was destined to be longer than anyone imagined.

The others?

Clair Barnes, aged thirty-five, from Falls Church, Virginia. Clair Barnes was a male. That's all newsmen could learn at first.

William Belk, aged forty-four, West Columbia, South Carolina, communications and record officer at the embassy. Veteran of twenty-two years in the Marines and Air Force. Two sons. His wife was to sue the Iranian government for $1 billion for kidnapping, false imprisonment and mental distress.

Robert Blucker, aged fifty-three, North Little Rock, Arkansas. An oil specialist, he had asked to transfer from duty in West Berlin. He arrived in Tehran a week before the takeover.

Donald Cooke, aged twenty-five, Memphis, Tennessee, a native of Long Island, New York. A graduate of Ohio State in geology. Vice consul. "Foreign service was always kind of in the back of his mind," his brother said.

William Daugherty, said to be thirty-three years old. Graduate of Oklahoma State. Served in the military, then the State Department. The militants said he admitted working for the CIA.

Lieutenant Cmdr. Robert Englemann U.S. Navy, aged thirty-three, Hurst, Texas. Naval attache. He had been in Tehran less than a week.

Corporal William Gallegos, aged twenty-two, Pueblo, Colorado, Marine, outdoorsman, karate expert. "So strong and brave and then so kind-hearted, patient and loving," said his mother.

Bruce German, aged forty-three, Kensington, Maryland, budget officer. He was to write: "Needless to say we have become rather bitter, disillusioned and frustrated because we believe that we are the victims of poor judgment and lack of foresight."

Duane Gillette, aged twenty-four, Columbia, Pennsylvania, four years in the Navy, communications specialist. Not married.

Alan Golacinski, aged twenty-nine, security officer.

John Graves, aged fifty-three, Reston, Virginia. Father of six. State Department since 1963 with service in Vietnam and Africa. Senior inspector in Tehran. A friend and former student said: "His depth and principles will serve him in good stead."

Warrant Officer Joseph Hall, aged thirty-one, Elyria, Ohio, grew up in Bend, Oregon. A jogger. His father said there had been nothing outstanding in his son's youth "other than running around raising hell on his Honda and driving around the Burger Hut and sneaking a few beers on the side."

Sergeant Kevin Hermening, aged twenty, Oak Creek, Wisconsin, the youngest hostage. His divorced and remarried mother, Mrs. Kenneth Timm, said her son had vowed to be "the best Marine that's ever been."

Donald Hohman, aged thirty-eight, West Sacramento, California, Marine medic. Wife and two sons.

Colonel Leland Holland, aged fifty-two, Fairfax, Virginia, Army Vietnam veteran. Married with six children.

Michael Howland, aged thirty-four, Alexandria, Virginia. With Laingen at the Foreign Ministry.

Charles A. Jones Jr., aged forty, Detroit, teletype operator. The only black not released. There was no explanation why.

Malcolm Kalp. Another CIA agent, the militants said.

Moorhead Kennedy Jr., aged forty-nine, Washington, D.C. Harvard Law. Expert on Islamic law. State Department economics specialist. Married, four children. His wife, Louisa would become well known on American television as the spokeswoman for FLAG, the Family Liaison Action Group.

Corporal Steve Kirtley, aged twenty-two, Little Rock. Marine. Two brothers and a sister also in the military.

Kathryn Koob, aged forty-three, Jesup, Iowa. Farm girl, graduate of Wartburg College, a Lutheran school, former church worker, then teacher. Joined State Department in 1969, served in Africa and Romania. Director of Iran-American Society in Tehran. She was working there that Sunday morning and kept a phone open to Washington. She was caught a day later. Her sister said: "She's the sort of person who says, 'Well, somebody's got to go. It might as well be me.'"

Steven Lauterbach, aged twenty-eight, Dayton, Ohio, graduate of Bowling Green with a master's from the University of Michigan. Sent to Tehran in March by State Department to help recover personal belongings of American evacuees.

Gary Lee, aged thirty-six, Falls Church, Virginia, business administrator at embassy for four years. Consular veteran, knew Hindi and other Middle Eastern languages.

Sergeant Paul Lewis, aged twenty-three, Homer, Illinois. Three-year Marine, homecoming king at high school. Arrived in Tehran the day before he became a hostage. Said his father: "I do know this: he believes in this country."

John W. Limbert Jr., aged thirty-seven, political officer.

Sergeant James Michael Lopez, aged twenty-two, Globe, Arizona. "100-plus Marine." In school ran a paper route, then went to band practice, then to football, all in an afternoon.

Sergeant Johnny McKeel Jr., aged twenty-seven, Balch Springs, Texas, graduate of school for foreign embassy guards. Would write: "I have seen better conditions in a dog pound."

Michael Metrinko, aged thirty-four, Olyphant, Pennsylvania, graduate of Georgetown University. Consul at Tabriz. Speaks Farsi.

Jerry Miele, aged forty-two, Mount Pleasant, Pennsylvania. Bachelor, eighteen years in State Department.

Sergeant Michael Moeller, aged twenty-eight, Loup City, Nebraska. Nine years a Marine. His wife said: "I knew when I married Mike that the Marine Corps was first and I've taken a back seat ever since."

Bert Moore, aged forty-five, Mount Vernon, Ohio, administration counselor at embassy. Militants said he was part of intelligence unit.

Richard Morefield, aged fifty-one, San Diego, two degrees, consul general. Wife, Dorothea, and two sons. Career diplomat. Kids called him "Papa Bear" because "He loves to growl. He wasn't the kind of father who would drag you along everywhere, but if you needed help with your homework, he would."

Captain Paul M. Needham, aged thirty, Bellevue, Nebraska. Air Force. On temporary duty in Iran to help Iranians get spare parts for American-supplied aircraft. Divorced.

Robert Ode, aged sixty-four, Sun City West, Arizona. Retired diplomat, oldest hostage. Arrived in Tehran on what was to have been a forty-five day temporary duty. Would write Washington Post: "I can only ask that you do everything possible to bring pressure on responsible leaders in our government to take prompt action to free us from this terrible situation."

Sergeant Gregory Persinger, aged twenty-two, Seaford, Delaware. Volunteered for a second tour in Iran.

Master Sgt. Regis Ragan, aged thirty-eight, Johnstown, Pennsylvania. Decorated Vietnam veteran in Army. In Iran five years.

Barry Rosen, aged thirty-six. Every drama has to have someone from Brooklyn. Rosen was it. Father of two.

William B. Royer Jr., aged forty-nine, West University Place, Texas. School teacher in Middle East since 1963. Among those who had been at the Iran-American Society.

Colonel Thomas Schaefer, aged fifty, Tacoma, Washington. Air Force. Military defense attache. In military almost thirty years. Married, one son.

Lieutenant Col. Charles Scott, aged forty-seven, Stone Mountain, Georgia. Army. On second tour in Iran. "I always wondered whether he'd stick up for himself, but once, when he was nine or ten years old, some boys called his younger sister 'four eyes' because she wore glasses. The next thing I knew, those boys were running down the street crying."

Donald A. Sharer, Chesapeake, Virginia. State Department employee.

Sergeant Rodney V. Sickmann, aged twenty-two, Krakow, Missouri. Father driver of concrete truck, mother carpet store employee. Called his girl friend two days before the takeover and said there might be trouble but asked her to tell his parents not to worry.

Sergeant Joseph Subic Jr., aged twenty-three, Redford Township, Michigan. Dropped out of high school and joined Army. Was to appear on film taken by militants criticizing role of United States in Iran.

Elizabeth Ann Swift, aged thirty-nine, Washington. Second-ranking political officer in embassy. One of released hostages said: "We called her 'Ann, Baby.' She was a cool lady."

Victor Tomseth, aged thirty-nine, McLean, Virginia. Graduate of University of Oregon, former Peace Corps worker in Iran, fluent in Nepalese, Thai and Farsi. Wife and two children were with him in Tehran until dependents of government employees were ordered home in December 1978. His mother said: "Victor is very calm and levelheaded. He's a diplomat." With Laingen.

Philip R. Ward, aged thirty, Culpeper, Virginia. Married, one child.

Americans, all. Hostages, all.

.   .   .

Right after the seizure, the State Department's Iran Working Group began calling the hostages' families daily, whether or not there was any news to report. One hundred of them were brought to Washington to meet and be personally briefed by President Carter. For the hostages, quarantined from each other like children with the mumps, there was to be no such period of getting acquainted.

In the first days, at least, conversation other than with their guards was not permitted. They had to request permission to go to the bathroom. The rest of the time they sat, hands bound. Some read, some wrote letters. They could smoke occasionally. Then the militants would untie their bonds. Men were allowed more cigarettes than women. One woman complained. A guard said it was bad for her health. "If you're so concerned about my health," she said, "turn me loose."

They were awakened each morning at 6:30, fed simple

but sufficient food three times during the day, then sent to bed at 10:00 P.M. on mattresses laid on the floor. Twice a week they could take showers.

Sergeant James Hughes, one of those later released, was badgered for information. If he didn't give it, the militants said, other hostages would be shot. "That goes with the job," he responded. The questions stopped. A Marine who refused to have his hands retied after a cigarette was overpowered. The hostages were bound and kept barefoot for their own good, their captors explained. If they escaped and got out on the streets, they would be killed by the mobs.

Each individual was in his or her own world, wondering what was to come, what the breaking point might be. The disciplined Marine, the disciplined school teacher; the dropout or the scholar; the Christian woman or the agnostic had only their own resources to draw on. Character would tell, but what it would tell remained to be seen.

Morefield's family had known of the potential dangers when he was offered the post in Tehran. The Morefields had a family meeting. "We all decided that if he wanted to go, he should go," said his fifteen-year-old son, Steven.

Steven saw his father in a brief moment on television the day after his capture.

Papa Bear, he said, "looked sort of mad."

46

*Can't keep a good man down. Chin-ups, anything to pass the time,
keep in trim. Some of the hostages grew better biceps.*

47

4

Atop the best-seller lists was The Complete Scarsdale Medical Diet *written in collaboration by Dr. Herman Tarnower, a noted physician of that New York community. Unbeaten Ohio State looked forward to adding Southern Cal to its string in the Rose Bowl. Chrysler's sales were down 44.5 percent, one reason being a Mazda three-door for $3,995. In Tehran it was . . .*

DAY 19

The crowds showed up every morning, regular as the milk. Their cries, when on camera, were clearly audible inside the embassy. When not posturing for the satellite feed into the U.S. evening news, they munched peanuts and gossiped. But one day it would be different. This was Ashura, the tenth day of the Moslem month of Muharram. It is a day that celebrates martyrdom. And it is, thus, a day which says much about why the crowds of Tehran reached a peak of frenzy, this time genuine, a day that goes far to explaining why they had shouted "Death to the Shah!" and "Death to America!"

Islam—the word means "submission," in this sense to the will of God—is the youngest of the world's great religions. It has 800 million believers, located mainly in a belt extending from the Philippines and Indonesia in the East through Pakistan, Russia, the Middle East and into Africa on the West. Moslems believe that Mohammad was the final prophet of God—Allah—having been preceded by Abraham and Jesus. Mohammad, who lived in what is now Saudi Arabia, died in 632 A.D. The struggle of his successors was bloody and led to a split in the faith. Eighty-five percent of the Moslems are followers of the Sunni branch of the religion. Most of the rest are of the Shiite branch. Iranians are largely Shiite. They are not, however, Arabs. Arabs are those who speak Arabic. The Iranians speak Farsi for the most part.

The split in the faith began almost immediately after Mohammad's death. The first caliph, or successor to the Prophet, was elected in accord with Arab tradition. A minority, who became the Shiites, believed the succession should fall to a direct descendant of the Prophet as an inheritor of his divinity, an imam, so-called, who is a go-between with Allah. The Shiites revered Ali, Mohammad's son-in-law and cousin, as an imam who should accordingly become caliph. He was eventually elected such but was assassinated six years later. His eldest son was poisoned. Meanwhile, the

caliphate had been moved to Damascus by the Sunnis. In the year 680, a group of Sunnis near Baghdad asked Hussein, Ali's second son and Mohammad's grandson, to leave the holy city of Mecca to become their imam. Yazid, the Sunni caliph, intercepted Ali and demanded he recognize Yazid as caliph. Hussein would not. He was left for ten days in the desert without water, then was butchered. His pieces were trod into the sand. Eleven succeeding imams were murdered. The twelfth disappeared. The Shiites believe he will reappear at the end of time as the messiah or Mahdi.

Hussein was slain on Ashura.

To atone for his death, Shiites on that day honor his martyrdom in pilgrimages to his tomb and Ali's. They also march through the streets flagellating themselves with chains. The Shiites attach great importance to martyrdom.

"Why should we be afraid?" Khomeini said after the embassy was seized. "We consider martyrdom a great honor!"

When Khomeini returned to Iran, he came not only as an ayatollah, a teacher, but as an imam, an intermediary with God. In exile he had called on his followers to wear white robes, the better to show their blood shed in the street fighting with the Shah's soldiers.

The Shiites believe as do other Moslems in the five obligations of Mohammad: pray five times daily, observe Islamic law—the Sharia, fast pay alms, and once in their lifetimes make a pilgrimage to Mecca to kiss the black stone inside the Kaaba, Islam's holiest shrone. Arabs believe it was built by Abraham. In addition, the Shiites place a high value on revenge. This colored their passionate hatred for the Shah. Personally, Khomeini believed the Shah was responsible for the deaths of his father and of his son. By extension the Iranians hated the United States, whose puppet they believed the Shah to be. Had he not been restored to the throne in 1953 by the CIA?

Americans viewing television film of Iranians beating themselves until they bled on the streets outside the embassy might have thought the scene barbaric, forgetting the agonies of the Passion play re-enactments of Christ's death. But to the Shiites, it was part of their tradition. And it had been Khomeini's genius to translate this emotion into representing the Shah as Caliph Yazid and SAVAK as those who had killed Hussein. And behind it all, "the Great Satan," the United States of America.

•   •   •

Ashura was not only a day of passion among Iran's thirty-eight million people, ninety-five percent of whom are Moslem. The whole Mohammaden world was stunned that

Traditions. They beat themselves with chains to remember one of their martyrs. It was eerie to American eyes, and they held American lives in their hands. ▷

Memory. While Americans were mourning Jack Kennedy, Iranians were in revolt. Half-a-million here commemorate the beginning of their revolution in 1963.△

IRAN, 'LAND OF THE ARYANS'

Known as Persia through most of its history, Iran is a country of diverse peoples, rich culture and stark physical contrasts—from the cool green landscapes that inspired the romantic poetry of Omar Khayyam, to forbidding wastelands of sand and salt that inspire nothing so much as dread.

THE LAND

More than twice the size of Texas, Iran comprises a high central plateau, the "dasht," ringed by mountain ranges. The tallest mountain, 18,386-foot-high Demavand, rises just north of Tehran, the capital and largest city. Except for a fertile belt along the Caspian Sea coast, Iran is semi-arid and historically has relied on extensive irrigation works for agriculture.

1 Azerbaijan
2 Kurdistan
3 Khuzestan
4 Balluchistan

THE HISTORY

The story of Persia stretches back 2,500 years, making it one of the world's oldest nations. Its zenith of power was reached more than two millennia ago.

About 1000 B.C., Aryan tribes from somewhere in central Asia migrated into Iran and dominated the indigenous people. One of the tribes, the Persians, eventually became supreme and by 500 B.C. had built an empire extending from India to Greece. But twenty years later their armies were defeated by the Greeks, and Persia began its decline.

Over the next 2,000 years, periods of conquest—by Greeks, Arabs, Seljuk Turks, Mongols—alternated with periods of autonomy. From the 1500s onward, Persia was independent under its own "shahs," or kings, although beginning in the 19th century it came under the strong influence of Russia and Western powers.

In 1921, cavalry officer Reza Khan seized power from the Qajar dynasty, eventually naming himself shah. The Allies forced Shah Reza off the throne in 1941 because of his links with Germany's Nazis, and replaced him with his twenty-one-year-old son, Mohammad Reza Pahlavi.

An anti-Western upheaval in 1953 toppled the young shah, but he was quickly restored to power in a countercoup aided by the United States. In 1979, another anti-shah revolution succeeded, and Iran was declared an Islamic Republic.

THE PEOPLE

About two-thirds of Iran's thirty-eight million people speak Persian or a Persian dialect as their main language. The others are a patchwork of linguistic and ethnic groups left behind by centuries of migration and conquest.

The largest groups are the Kurds and Azerbaijanis of the northwest, each totaling some five million people. The Kurds, a clannish mountain people, have rebelled periodically against the Persians, including the current government. Both they and the Azerbaijanis, who speak a Turkish dialect, briefly seceded from Iran under Soviet sponsorship after World War II.

The Baluchis of the southeast and the Turkomans of the northeast also have resisted central Persian control in recent years. In Iran's southwestern corner, a large Arabic-speaking population has long agitated against Persian rule. The tribal Lurs and Bakhtiaris of the southwestern mountains are believed to be remnants of aboriginal Persians who did not mix with other ethnic strains.

In some cases, ethnic differences are sharpened by religion. Ninety percent of Iranians adhere to the Shiite branch of Islam, but the Kurds, Turkomans and Baluchis are members of the rival Sunni sect.

RESOURCES

In 1908, a British mining engineer discovered oil in Khuzistan, in Iran's southwest. By the late 1970s, Iran had become the world's second largest oil exporter, shipping out 5.7 million barrels a day. But the 1978-79 revolution reduced production to a trickle.

Iran has proven oil reserves of some fifty-eight billion barrels, twice as much as the United States, and it has been a major producer of natural gas. But its sands and mountains have yielded few other natural resources.

THE ECONOMY

Shah Mohammad Reza Pahlavi launched a massive modernization program in the 1960s, one accelerated by the revenues from the large oil price increases of the 1970s.

The ambitious development plans, coupled with huge, non-productive spending on the military, disrupted the traditionally agricultural economy. A country once self-sufficient in wheat and other grain became an importer of such staples. Serious inflation became chronic, and the influx of rural people into overburdened cities caused major social dislocations.

Iran's factories produce cotton and woolen textiles, tobacco products, cement, brick, refined copper, chemicals, leather goods and other products, but little is exported. Traditional industries—such as caviar and rug-making—remain important.

same day when a Saudi who proclaimed himself the Mahdi stormed the holy of holies, the Kaaba, with a group of heavily armed followers and captured it.

The leader, a long-haired man in his twenties, shabbily dressed, had been loitering in the courtyard of the Kaaba for several days, mingling with the pilgrims on their homage to the shrine—the hajj. About 4:00 A.M. November 21, the day before Thanksgiving in the United States, as the muzein was summoning the faithful for morning prayer, the man rushed into the Kaaba. With him were several hundred others, armed with pistols and Uzis, Israeli submachine guns. Saudi Arabia immediately closed off news reports, but as many as one hundred people were reported killed. Rumors flashed through the Moslem world.

About 1:00 P.M. in Pakistan, coverage of a Pakistani-Indian cricket match was interrupted by a news bulletin reporting the seizure in Mecca. Somehow a rumor began spreading that the United States and Israel were behind the attack. Crowds began gathering outside the U.S. Embassy in Islamabad. The next day, shortly after noon, "all hell broke loose," according to an American newswoman in the embassy. The crowds began setting fire to cars and then stormed the embassy. About ninety people in the embassy were rushed into a special steel-lined room on the third floor which was the communications center. As the embassy burned, those in the room began choking and dripping with sweat in the parboiling heat. A Marine, Cpl. Steve Crowley, aged nineteen, of Selden, New York, was shot in the head while guarding the roof and was carried into the room, dying. After more than four hours, the smoke and heat became overpowering and Marines led everyone to the roof. By then, Pakistani soldiers, who had been summoned at the onset of the attack, began arriving. After the fires were extinguished, the bodies of Warrant Officer Bryan Ellis and two Pakistani clerks were found in the ruins. American legations in Turkey, Bangladesh and India were also attacked by Moslem demonstrators. It seemed to be open season on Uncle Sam. Khomeini was jubilant.

"It is a great joy for us to learn about the uprising against the United States. Borders should not separate hearts."

．　　　．　　　．

Exactly what Islamic laws pertained to the seizure in Iran was open to dispute. Zaki Badawi, Egyptian director of the Islamic Cultural Center in London, believed the demand for the return of the Shah was consistent with Moslem legality. Under Islamic law, "no one is above the law and is supreme. If a crime is committed by a ruler, an emperor, he is as liable to punishment for it as the meanest and commonest of his subjects." The late King Saud of Saudi Arabia was banished by an Islamic court and exiled for drinking, gambling and womanizing.

Islam, at the same time, "teaches love, tolerance and mercy," said Anwar Sadat. "This is not Islam," Sadat said of the seizure. Badawi agreed.

"There is no basis in Islam for this. Islam does not justify the taking of hostages, and it (the Sharia) also clearly states that one person cannot be punished for the crimes of another."

A Cairo professor said Khomeini's "evil hunger for the death of a sick man is a towering crime under Islamic law" which "considers any sick or dying person with extreme humility."

Ruhollah Ramanzani, an Iranian scholar at the University of Virginia, said that by Moslem law, "if an undesirable individual enters into the Moslem domain, then that person must be protected and escorted to the boundaries of the domain to let him out safely."

A contrasting viewpoint was given by Mohammed Javad Bahonar, a forty-six-year-old member of Khomeini's Revolutionary Council. His words evoked both Islamic law and the xenophobia Iranians have felt for centuries as the crossroads and doormat of an unending line of conquerors.

"The United States insulted the Iranian national honor," he said, "by giving the Shah a visa. The ex-dictator represents all the pain, torture, humiliation, deprivation and repression suffered for decades by our nation. And just at a time when Iranians believed Wasington at least tacitly recognized this fact, the ex-tyrant triumphantly enters New York. What this nation has suffered at the hands of the Shah is no less serious than what the Jews suffered at the hands of the Nazis. Then, when our turn comes, your measuring stick suddenly shrinks. With weapons supplied by you and under the supervision of your military advisers, hundreds of innocent women, children and men were being mowed down every day.

To the Shiite mentality, the hostages were symbols of vengeance. They were hostage to a religious background, a history and a man. They were also hostage to a revolutionary zeal that rallied the patriotism of many diverse people against a universal enemy, the United States.

As President Carter ordered a second carrier to the Gulf, Khomeini mixed both retribution and his nation's new-found pride when he declared that if the United States struck, "The hostages will be killed."

Sadat said Khomeini was "a lunatic."

But to many of his people, long accustomed to political activism among their clergy, Khomeini was not only an ayatollah. He was an imam, an incarnation of the descendants of the Prophet. His will was as Allah's.

The Man from Qum. They Ayatollah Ruhollah Khomeini, frail and weak, aging, his word is law.

CIA, PENTAGON, UN
VIETNAM WOUNDED
IRAN WILL BURY YO

DOWN WITH carter

5

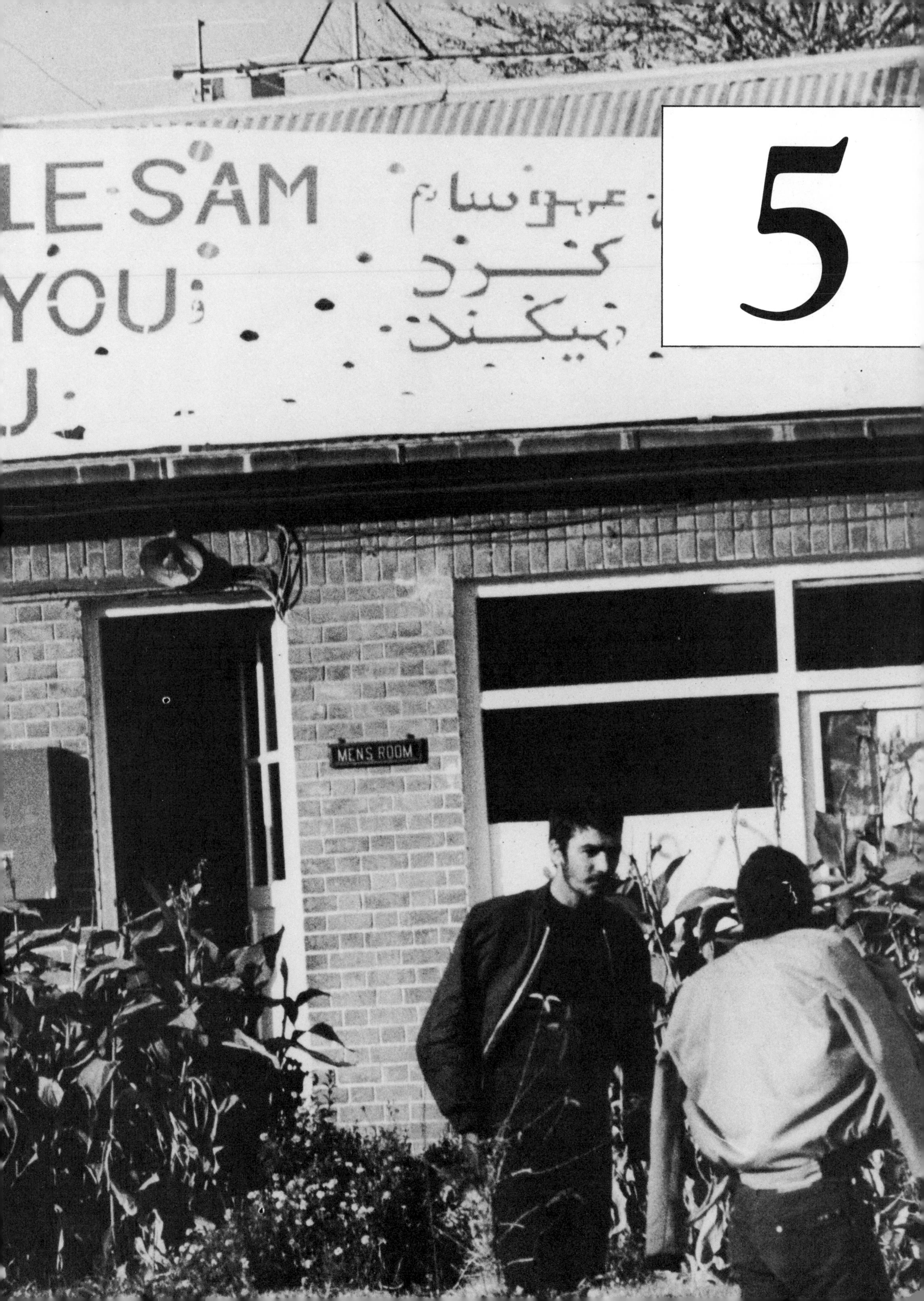

In New York the Museum of Modern Art put on a special exhibit to celebrate its fiftieth anniversary. Mexico said the Shah could not return there on leaving his New York hospital. And at the United Nations, U.S. Ambassador Donald F. McHenry said Americans were "seething" at Iran, where it was...

DAY 28

Even older then the Koran, the holy book of the Moslems, is the Bible. In its second book, Exodus, is laid out a stern precept of Judaic-Christian justice: "Eye for eye, tooth for tooth, hand for hand, foot for foot."

But if the United States sought justice at the United Nations, the International Court at the Hague in Holland and in world opinion, only Khomeini could give it, and he did not see eye to eye. So Americans sought revenge on the Iranians in their midst.

A Chicago night club owner fired five Iranian waiters. Trustees at Greenville, South Carolina, Technical Community College voted to expel 104 Iranian students, then reversed themselves. An Islamic center in New York was burned. Left behind was a sign: "Free Americans or you will die." Four Iranians on a holiday in Mexico from the United States were refused re-entry. A New Jersey bus operator fired six Iranian drivers. "I won't take, I can't take, Americans being held hostage by these degenerates."

Judy Blucker, whose brother was prisoner in the embassy, said: "I got over my 'Send in the Marines' syndrome the first day."

Other hostage family members were privately enraged at the lack of government precautions to protect the embassy. "I'm so bitter I could scream," said Louisa Kennedy.

In Washington, Jimmy Carter kept to the White House, grim faced, trying to effect what ever diplomacy could do. Emissaries to the NATO powers tried to get them to follow U.S. sanctions against Iran, but only West Germany fully complied. Carter acted decisively when he could. Awakened in the middle of the night to be shown a news service story reporting that Iranians were going to withdraw their money from American banks, he had a freeze order ready by the time the banks opened that morning.

One thing had also been decided. The United States would not go to war. Instead of a gala announcement of his campaign for re-election, Carter held only a brief, somber address in the White House.

"I have made some mistakes, and I have learned from them," he said. "I carry some scars, and I carry them with pride."

One moment of cheer was provided the Carter camp by Ted Kennedy. Sitting through a routine interview on television in San Francisco, the senator was asked if the United States shouldn't reward the Shah's long alliance with that country by granting him sanctuary.

Kennedy, who once was photographed smilingly shaking the Shah's hand, said the ex-ruler had operated "one of the most violent regimes in the history of mankind" and had stolen "umpteen billions of dollars."

"I was tired," the senator said afterwards, but the nation fumed.

"It's not fatal, but he can't afford many more like it," said the campaign aide.

"Kennedy hasn't lost it," said a Carter assistant. "But he's done the next best thing. He's given us an even start, and in an even start we have all the cards."

•   •   •

In Iran, voters almost unanimously approved a new constitution, in effect granting Khomeini rule for life. His office announced that the violence in Mecca was the result of "criminal U.S. imperialism."

In Paris, Shariar Mustapha Chafik, the Shah's thirty-four-year-old nephew, was assassinated on orders by the head of Iran's Revolutionary Tribunal.

All the focus of all this, the Shah?

At 4:00 A.M. December 2, the Shah left the hospital through a sub-basement and was flown to Lackland Air Force Base in San Antonio, Texas. Mexico had reneged on a promise to take him back, and the United States searched the world for someone willing to take him in. Meanwhile, he was installed in a two-bedroom suite. He occasionally walked his Great Dane about the grounds, watched his wife play tennis and chatted on the phone with old friends, including Kissinger.

He was both an ill and bitter man. He had written a book, soon to be published, entitled *A Response to History.* In it, he accused the Carter Administration of helping to oust him. He said that Air Force Gen. Robert Huyser had met with Iranian generals to talk them out of a coup to keep the Shah just before his downfall.

The Shah quoted an Iranian general: "Huyser threw the emperor out of the country like a dead mouse."

At home. While American hostages languished in captivity, their fleeting images ticking off day after day on television, the American political scene flickered on and off.

...rom The People o
Houston, TX.

6

AMERICAN HOSTAGES
U.S. EMBASSY
260 TAKHTE JAMSHID AVE.
TEHRAN, IRAN

Millions of Americans added a new address to their Christmas card lists: U.S. Embassy, Box 50, 260 Taleghani Avenue, Tehran, Iran. The national tree in Washington was dimmed save for a single star at the top. It was Christmas...

DAY 52

For a brief moment the Peace of Christ did what words and warships had failed to do: open the steel gates of the embassy.

Three American clergymen—one a black, the other two pacifists—were allowed inside the embassy to hold Christmas services for the captives. So was a nine-foot Christmas tree sent from Seattle. And 90,000 Christmas cards of some three million sent from across the United States.

There were tears. Carols. Cookies. Incredulity that the Tampa Bay Buccaneers had made the National Football League playoffs. Who was in the Rose Bowl? The man of God knew Southern Cal was one team. He didn't know Ohio State was the other.

The three clergymen had been invited to Tehran by Khomeini. He had obviously not picked at random. One was the Rev. William Sloane Coffin, pastor of New York's Riverside Church and a former CIA agent. He left the agency to finish divinity studies at Yale University in 1956. He was a prominent opponent of the Vietnam war. In 1968 he was tried with Dr. Benjamin Spock and three others for conspiring to counsel draft evaders. His conviction was overturned on appeal. In 1972 he visited Hanoi with other anti-war activists and returned with three war prisoners released by the North Vietnamese.

The second minister was the Rev. M. William Howard of Princeton, New Jersey, elected head of the National Council of Churches in 1978 at the age of thirty-two. A black, he grew up in Americus, Georgia, near Jimmy Carter's hometown of Plains.

The third was a Catholic, the Rev. Thomas J. Gumbleton, aged forty-nine, Auxiliary Bishop of Detroit. He was a prominent pacifist and opponent of the arms race. he favored conscientious objection to military service and was often at odds with his church as president of pacifist groups for Pax Christi U.S.A. and Bread for the World.

Before leaving New York, Coffin criticized Carter's handling of the hostage crisis. His effort to get the United Nations to impose economic sanctions was, he said, "highly reminiscent of Lyndon Johnson's bombing of North Viet-

nam; it puts iron up the spines of the other side."

"Maybe something will happen when we get there," Gumbleton said before boarding a plane for Iran.

"We scream about the hostages, but few Americans hear the screams of tortured Iranians," Coffin commented.

In honor of the occasion, the militants removed the hostages' bonds. For many of the captives it was their first chance since November 4 to talk to Americans other than themselves.

The clergymen had wanted to meet with all the hostages as a group. The militants felt this would be a security risk. So they met in small groups. "We sang together, prayed together and shared the Eucharist together," said Gumbleton.

Coffin, who met with sixteen of the captives, said "There were tears in their eyes. There were tears in our eyes. I pray to God they will be released just as soon as possible."

Howard, a Baptist, told a news conference later some of the hostages "were not interested in worship per se." They were more interested to know what the scores were back home, who was playing whom in football.

Their captors had warned the hostages not to delve into politics. When one of the Americans asked Howard about the Rose Bowl, he snapped to his guard: "Or is that too political a question?" Howard overheard another hostage mutter to the guards: "What do you guys know?" About ten of the hostages he saw were "clearly rebellious," Howard said. When a hostage asked Gumbleton if Kennedy were still running for President, a guard intervened.

Coffin met with Barry Rosen, the press attache from Brooklyn who appeared downcast at first. "His face lit up when I said I had a kiss from Alexander," his young son. "I had met his wife and Alexander in New York, and she had told the boy, 'Kiss Mr. Coffin, and he'll take your kiss to Daddy.'"

There was a joyful reunion between Kathryn Koob and Elizabeth Ann Swift, the two women hostages who had apparently been kept apart. Later Coffin talked with Laingen at the Foreign Ministry.

"In a way he was like our government. He was so preoccupied with what was happening to the hostages that, for all his knowledge and love of Iran, he was incapable of taking his mind off them and thinking how we could bridge the gap. Then we spoke to the mullahs, and they were so preoccupied with the Shah and his wrongdoing that they were unable to think of the hostages. There is a complete lack of understanding between the two sides."

A Kiss of Peace, a kiss from Alexander, and Christmas at the embassy was over.

Yellow ribbons. The national symbol taken from a popular song which says, "Please come home to me."

When the gates of the compound closed behind them the clergymen counted up heads. They agreed they had met with forty-three hostages. The militants had said they were holding forty-nine. Where were the other six? Or was it seven?

The militants said six of their captives had not wanted to attend religious services. "Even if you were a confirmed atheist, you would want to see visiting Americans and pass on messages to your families," said one Tehran diplomat. Perhaps Daugherty, Ahern and Kalp, accused of being CIA agents, were being kept separately. But Ahern was a devout Catholic. He would not have turned down a chance to see a priest.

The State Department said it was a "very cruel numbers game."

*   *   *

The United States in the meantime had taken its case to the highest court in the world, the International Court of Justice, an arm of the United Nations sitting in an imposing palace in The Hague. U.S. Attorney General Benjamin Civiletti had made the opening plea.

The fifteen justices—no nation may be respresented by more than one—are elected for nine-year terms by the United Nations. They are paid $66,500 a year tax free to hear international disputes. But only forty-three of the U.N.'s 151 members had agreed to accept their jurisdiction. The American acceptance had been conditional. Since its founding in 1945, the court had made fourteen final judgments. It had prestige but not power. A nation could simply declare an issue a domestic matter and ignore the tribunal.

The American position was that Iran had violated four treaties which it had signed, including a guarantee of the safety of foreign diplomats and an acceptance of the court's jurisdiction. After four days of deliberation, the court directed Iran to free the hostages.

Iran had boycotted the arguments, saying the hostages were an internal matter.

Ghotbzadeh, as mercurial as a sandstorm, was now saying the matter might best be decided by an international tribunal instead of Iranian spy trials. Sean MacBride, an Irish winner of the Nobel Peace Prize, was mentioned as one of the panelists. The panel would hear evidence of American spying and manipulation in Iran.

On the other hand, said the prime minister, if the United Nations were to agree to impose sanctions against Iran, the hostages would be tried as spies after all.

"The Americans keep interpreting every reasonable gesture we make as a sign of weakness," he said. "We offer a tribunal instead of a trial, we allow the Christian priests in to visit the embassy, and the Americans reply with talk of sanctions. If they keep trying to put this sort of pressure on us, then let's forget the tribunal. Let's have an ordinary trial and try them all for being spies."

Ordinary trials under the Khomeini regime had had a rather predictable outcome: execution.

*   *   *

The day after Christmas is probably the most widely observed undeclared holiday in America. So it was in 1979.

But in Russia, always an unknown in the hostage equation, it was a time for action. The Russian bear had too long tolerated the bumblings of its puppet in Afghanistan. Mountain tribesmen who seemed born to fight whomever sat in authority in Kabul were back at their ancient ways. The bear swiped its paw, arranging the assassination of President Hafizullah Amin and replaced him with a more dependable ruler, Babrak Karmal. Soviet troops in large numbers began moving into Afghanistan.

There was now another unknown in the equation.

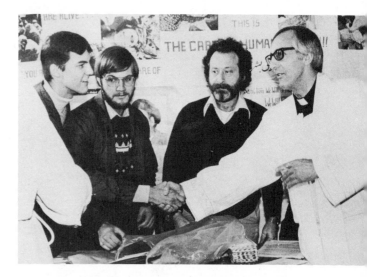

Visits. In lieu of freedom, visits from free Americans, here the Rev. Thomas J. Gumbleton, Catholic auxiliary bishop of Detroit, with hostages, Christmas morning, 1979.

Their first Christmas. A hostage reads from the Bible. The embassy is their home, their church.

THE PUEBLO INCIDENT

They had dozens of Americans held hostage. It was an election year in the United States. The president took the matter to the United Nations. He sent a carrier task force into the area.

There was delicate diplomatic maneuvering—even double talk. And, finally, freedom.

The year was 1968, and those hostages were in North Korea, not Iran.

But the Iranian hostages crisis had an uncanny resemblance to that lesson in history—the eleven-month hostage crisis in North Korea.

The American intelligence ship USS Pueblo was seized by North Korea on January 23, 1968. One American was shot and later died. Eighty-two others were taken prisoner.

Although there were differences, there were many similarities between the incidents in Korea and Iran.

In both cases, the United States was unable—either militarily or diplomatically—to influence events in a small nation holding Americans by force.

President Lyndon B. Johnson in 1968—and President Jimmy Carter in 1980—ruled out a quick military rescue.

Both hostage takings were denounced in Washington as clear violations of international law. And both lingered for days, weeks and finally months.

The release of the Pueblo crew centered on delicate diplomatic maneuvering aimed at allowing both countries to save face.

After twenty-seven days of talk, spanning eleven months, American and North Korean representatives came to an agreement in mid-December. The crewmen, along with the body of their colleague, were released.

As part of the deal, Maj. Gen. Gilbert H. Woodward, the chief U.S. negotiator, signed a lengthy document admitting that the USS Pueblo had entered North Korean waters to spy, as North Korea had claimed all along. In the document, the United States apologized.

But in a separate statement, cleared earlier by the North Korean representative, Woodward renounced the first document.

With the ink barely dry, Woodward declared the United States "could not apologize for actions which we did not believe took place . . . and my signature will not and cannot alter the fact."

The release of the Pueblo crew ended months of frustration at the State Department, White House and Pentagon.

Dean Rusk, then secretary of State, told Americans one hundred days into the Pueblo crew's captivity that negotiations were at a stalemate. And the Americans had been taken inland, making a military rescue all but impossible.

Like President Carter in the Iranian situation, President Johnson sent a carrier task force in the area of confrontation. Carter sent the USS Kitty Hawk to the Indian Ocean. Johnson moved the USS Enterprise off the North Korean coast.

Carter eventually launched a top-secret rescue mission. But it was scrubbed in the predawn darkness of April 25 because three helicopters had been disabled by malfunctions.

Within days of the hostage crisis, Carter, like Johnson a dozen years earlier, took the matter to the U.N. Security Council. But, like the Iranians, the North Koreans declared they would pay no attention to what the United Nations said.

But there also were differences.

The United States and North Korea had no official diplomatic relations as had existed between the governments in Washington and Tehran.

But ironically, in the Pueblo case, the United States and North Korea were able to continue a direct dialogue, using the armistice talks at Panmunjom as a vehicle. There were no direct talks, as far as was publicly revealed, between U.S. and Iranian government officials over the hostages.

While the United States has received almost unanimous support in the world community, including demands by the United Nations and World Court that the hostages be released, no such world opinion was evident in the Pueblo case.

And the hostages in Iran were enmeshed in Iran's internal power struggles. U.S. negotiators trying to get the Pueblo crew released had only to deal with a single, authoritarian regime.

7

"Kramer vs. Kramer" and "10," which made Bo Derek a figure to be considered, were 1979's box office winners. Alfred Hitchcock, aged eighty, was knighted. Richard Rodgers, composer of "South Pacific" and "Oklahoma!" died at age seventy-seven. U.N. Secretary-General Kurt Waldheim headed for Tehran where it was . . .

DAY 58

The United Nations lives in a tower of glass on New York's East River, but like most residents of such glass houses, it is often reluctant to throw stones. So it was with Iran.

As diplomats themselves, the delegates needed no seminars on the necessity for diplomatic immunity. But the Third World majority felt more aligned with the little guy in any dispute than with the biggest boy on the block.

The Security Council ended its work for 1979 with a tentative vote. By 11-0, with Russia and Czechoslovakia abstaining, the council voted to give Tehran until January 7 to release the hostages. If it did not, the council would consider imposing sanctions. In the meantime, Waldheim decided to go to Iran himself to see what a little courtly old world diplomacy might do.

He was in for a shock. Iranian newspapers greeted him on January 1 with an old photograph of the urbane Austrian kissing the hand of the Shah's sister, Princess Ashraf. An Iranian jostled up to the secretary-general.

"Is this you, Mr. Waldheim, kissing the hand of a prostitute?"

Ghotbzadeh rolled out no red carpets. "There is no invitation for the secretary-general's visit," he said. "He is coming here on his own." In Qum, Khomeini confided: "I don't trust this man."

Lacking leaders to talk to, Waldheim went through the age-old diplomatic traditions of laying a wreath at the tomb of an honored dead, in this case Ayatollah Mahmoud Taleghani. When his limousine pulled into Behesht-Zahra cemetery, he was greeted with clamoring mobs. They shouted the customary death threats to the Shah and Jimmy Carter and waved in his face photographs of relatives they claimed SAVAK had slain. Waldheim, fearing for his safety, locked his door and commanded his driver: "Go, go, go!" He went.

Waldheim walked a proper line of neutrality. He referred to the captives not as hostages but as "the personnel in the American Embassy." But when visiting a rehabilitation center for SAVAK victims that had once been the secret police's officer club, he was brought a five-year-old boy and told his arms had been amputated by SAVAK in front of his father to force him to talk. Deeply moved, Waldheim held the boy for a moment, then said: "You may be assured that what happened under the Shah's regime will be the subject of an inquiry."

At the embassy itself, attendance had fallen off. A local Iranian said the militants "know that they aren't going to get back the Shah, but they don't know how to get out of it. They desperately need Khomeini to settle the matter, or they need something new to keep it going, to bring the crowds back to the embassy."

As if to oblige, the militants demanded that Laingen be turned over to them. The chargé and his two colleagues had been under house arrest all this time at the Foreign Ministry but had exercise privileges and some knowledge of what was going on in the outside world. Ghotbzadeh, who was running for president in an election scheduled for January 25, told the students no. So they said they were considering trying Lt. Col. Roeder for war crimes when he was a pilot in Vietnam.

After three days of getting nowhere, Waldheim flew home. Iran was one problem. There was also Afghanistan.

On his return, Waldheim told the Security Council that "enforcement" against Iran would only stiffen their resistance. The Council twice postponed voting sanctions. On January 13 it finally did so, ten of the fifteen members being in favor. Russia vetoed the resolution. The United States said it would enact the sanctions unilaterally.

Diplomacy had exhausted both the secretary-general and another hope for rescue.

Show of strength. Factory workers outside the embassy in support of students within. President Carter and the Shah were burned in effigy. ◬

◄ *Even the United Nations is not immune from the wrath of the people of Iran. Secretary-General Kurt Waldheim escapes in a helicopter from angry crowds in Tehran.*

69

8

Two undefeated teams came to grief in the New Year's bowl games. Southern Cal upset Ohio State 17-16 in the Rose Bowl. In the Orange Bowl it was Oklahoma 24, previously unbeaten Florida State 7. The news did not get over the wall in Tehran where it was . . .

DAY 59

There was another mob hollering defiance in the streets of Tehran as the new year began. This time the marchers were Afghanis living in Iran. Their target was also an embassy, but this time the Russian. The cause of their anger: the Russian invasion of their homeland.

Some youths tore down the Russian flag and burned it. They ran up a white flag in its place, a white banner saying, "There is no God but Allah."

The demonstrators were pushed back by revolutionary militiamen carrying submachine guns, a show of force absent November 4. The militiamen shouted through bullhorns for the demonstrators to go to the American Embassy and protest there against "imperialism."

Some did.

Russians get theirs. Iranians stormed the Russian Embassy in Tehran, protesting the invasion of Afghanistan. The red flag was ripped to tatters.

9

In India, Indira Gandhi was making a remarkable comeback to political leadership. Colonel Shorty Powers, once the voice of NASA, died at age fifty-seven. It was he who marked the countdowns in the glory days of liftoffs. The countdown went on and on in Tehran, and on January 23 Ayatollah Khomeini entered a hospital with a heart ailment, it also being . . .

DAY 81

To Khomeini the paradigm of rule occurred in the 7th century, under the Imam Ali who governed the bodies and spirits of his people with a purity inspired by Allah. He would renounce the false and evil trappings of a modern state, imported from the evil West by a satanic Shah, and create reborn an Islamic republic. Women would clothe their bodies in the traditional dark cloak, the chador, and return to the hearth. Music would stop. Men would live by God's laws as he, the Ayatollah, saw them.

It was the vision of a lifelong mystic.

Speaking in a voice barely above a mumble, his words chartered the fate of a nation no less than had the Shah's. The new constitution established an elected presidency and parliament but above them was a "guardian council" to determine that Islamic law was observed. And overseeing them all was a faqih, the holiest man of the nation. The constitution did not name him. It did not have to. Khomeini would be faqih.

He was also Savior of the Generations, Defeater of the Oppressors, Imam of the Age. This last title did not sit easily with a rival, Ayatollah Seyed Kazem Sharietmadari. The twelfth imam would indeed come one day, he said, "but not in a Boeing 747."

If Khomeini's origins did not seem to have marked him for temporal power, they were consonant with the life of a holy man. He was born either in 1900 or 1902, versions differ, in the town of Khomein, about 180 miles south of Tehran. His family name was Mustafavi. He later adopted the name of his birthplace. His father was an ayatollah. Many of his ancestors had been clerics.

"It was taken for granted we would all follow religious education," said Khomeini's brother, Ayatollah Morteza Pasandideh. "His brothers were very outgoing, but he kept to himself. He never participated in any of the family gatherings. We never had any idea he would become a leader."

His father was shot in 1901, apparently in a dispute with a local landlord. One version is that this had been ordered by Reza Shah who was then still an obscure soldier.

At the age of thirteen he began wearing a black turban, indicating he was a descendant of Mohammed. He became a teacher of ethics, philosophy and mysticism who "never liked to chat about ordinary things or waste his time," a former student recalled. "We had to get to the point, and when he made a decision, he left the room."

"The trouble with talking to him is that you always run up against a wall called God," said an American scholar who has had long interviews with with Khomeini. His absorption in religious matters left little room for the business of the world beyond. In 1964 he attacked the Shah for granting diplomatic immunity to United States military advisers and was exiled to Turkey. The Shah, he said, "Is such a filthy and impure being that, were he to touch the ocean, it would become polluted." Khomeini settled in Iraq for the next fourteen years and taught at an Islamic school.

"We forgot all about him, and didn't think of him again until he went to Paris," a kinsman recalled. That was in 1978. By then the Shah was in trouble, and the Ayatollah's tape recorded messages from exile struck a harmonious chord back home. They were angry messages.

"What drives Khomeini, what has kept him alive, is his desire for vengeance," said a British Iranian scholar. His elder son, Mustafa, then forty-nine, died in 1978 possibly at the hands of SAVAK. Khomeini did not forget. "He is a very bitter man, much more vindictive than the Shah," the Briton said.

For forty years he had accused the Pahlavi dynasty of corruption and foreign domination. And suddenly the Shah was gone, and Khomeini stood unchallenged. His faith was puritanical. His writings outlined hair-splitting codes for life, even covering how one should eat the meat of a sodomized camel, if an underground pamphlet of his teachings printed in Paris is to be believed. The impact of his philosophy was easily accepted in a country where church and state are one. His deep suspicion of foreigners epitomized that of his countrymen, yet this was a world that was all but unknown to him.

To Western ears, his pronouncements often seemed to confirm Sadat's diagnosis of lunacy. But Khomeini was primarily speaking to his own people, albeit through such Western innovations as tape recorders, radio and television.

"When he seems most crazy to us, he appears most exemplary to the Iranian people," said Richard Falk, professor of foreign affairs at Princeton University. "That suggests you would have to say all of Iran is crazy."

Soon after Khomeini returned, banks and heavy indus-

The Face. In the deepness of the eyes, in the white beard, in the halo-like turban, faith of Iranians, bewilderment for America.

try were nationalized. Women were segregated from men at beaches, public facilities and classrooms except for the universities. Alcohol and Western music were banned. Such music "dulls the mind because it involves pleasure and ecstasy," said the Ayatollah.

"Even the music of Bach, Beethoven, Verdi?" asked Italian journalist Oriana Fallaci. "I do not know those names," Khomeini replied.

Khomeini is, said another ayatollah, "a good wrecker but a bad builder."

He settled in Qum, a holy city of a quarter of a million people where there are eighteen seminaries. The ultimate seat of government became Khomeini's one-story, four-room house on a side street of the dusty provincial city. Militiamen stood guard at either end of the blockaded thoroughfare. The great and the small alike awaited on the Ayatollah's presence in an anteroom lit by a bare overhead bulb. Iranian Radio and Television kept equipment on permanent standby to broadcast any of his announcements. The house had four single service phone lines. The Ayatollah had no hesitancy about using the electronic media. But not phones. His son, Seyed Ahmed, did that for him.

Khomeini practiced the asceticism he preached. His diet was limited to rice, bean curd, yogurt, raw onions, a little mutton. Because of his heart condition, he only worked a few hours a day.

"The country should be content with a simple way of life," said Hamid Enayat, an Oxford scholar. His example should be the standard for all Iran."

An American said Khomeini "has an earthy sense of justice. He is for private property, cheap meat and electricity and plenty of water. That makes him an Iranian populist. He has a George Wallace sense of how people think."

In the sudden shift of gears, as though a speeding car had suddenly been thrown into reverse, Iran became a confusion. The Kentucky Fried Chicken stand in the Tehran suburbs was still open. Television still broadcast old American movies occasionally, but there were also televised instructions on how to handle a submachine gun. Tall buildings stood unfinished as construction stopped almost totally. New laws permitted men to have four wives, rescinding a 1967 statute restricting polygamy.

More seriously, the nationalistic appeals of the revolutionaries has whetted regional appetites for autonomy. When eleven demonstrators supporting Ayatollah Shariat-Madari were executed by Khomeini militiamen in Tabriz, fighting broke out anew. Kurds ambushed some government police. An oil tank explosion in Abadan was blamed by some in Iranian Arabs. Shiites fought Sunni Moslems in Bandar-e Lengeh. Sixty-six people died.

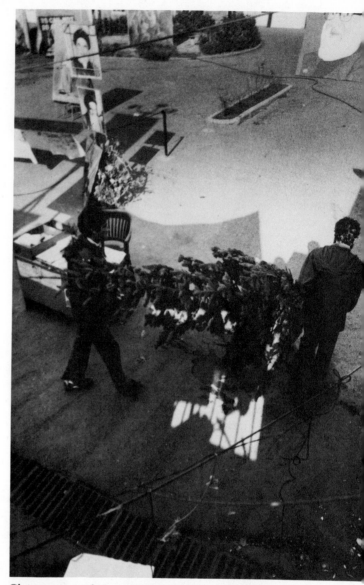

Christmas exported. Carts of Christmas cards and bales of Christmas trees piled up at Tehran airport as symbols of support. One tree from Seattle made it to the embassy.

Khomeini has masterfully orchestrated the hostages into a test of patriotism. His hatred and vengeance had, for the moment at least, defined national purpose. But he had also made the hostages a domestic issue as well as an international purpose. But he had also made the hostages a domestic issue as well as an international one. The longer the crisis continued, the more important the question became: who was in charge—the militants, the government, or Khomeini?

He was not kept long in the hospital. But the game he was playing was not for the weak of heart.

ABOLHASSAN BANI-SADR

Abolhassan Bani-Sadr emerged as the most conciliatory of top Iranian officials in trying to end the hostage crisis. But he was caught with the hostages in a political storm swirling over revolutionary Iran.

The forty-six-year-old Bani-Sadr's power may have peaked January 25, 1980, the day he was elected first president of the Islamic Republic of Iran by an overwhelming popular vote. Since then, he has been locked in a struggle with Moslem clergymen who have gradually chipped away at his position in a bid to take full command of the revolution.

The conservative clerics distrust what they see a leftist, Western tendencies of foreign-educated technocrats. Bani-Sadr, despite his flawless revolutionary and religious credentials, falls into that category.

Iran's president was born the son of an ayatollah, a high-ranking clergyman of Iran's Shiite Moslem sect. He was educated in economics and theology at the University of Tehran, and later continued his studies during more than a decade of exile in France.

In the early 1950s, Bani-Sadr became active in a Tehran student movement opposed to Shah Mohammad Reza Pahlavi's regime. In 1963, he was wounded when the Shah's forces put down violent anti-government protests in Tehran. After spending four months in jail for his activities, he fled to France.

While abroad, he published two books depicting his homeland as an economic and military fiefdom of the United States, and calling for greater Iranian economic self-reliance.

When Ayatollah Ruhollah Khomeini, symbol of the anti-Shah position, went to France, Bani-Sadr became one of his closest associates. He returned to Tehran in revolutionary triumph with Khomeini in February 1979.

Bani-Sadr was named as one of the dozen or so members of the secret ruling body, the Revolutionary Council. He also became provisional finance minister and foreign minister.

As economics chief, he said he wanted to reshape the Iranian economy in an Islamic mold. Among other measures, he nationalized banks and outlawed bank interest, in keeping with Moslem principles.

In the days following the seizure of the U.S. Embassy, Bani-Sadr's bespectacled, mustachioed face became familiar to millions of Americans as he searched for a way to negotiate a resolution to the crisis. But instead he was denounced by hard-liners as weak and pro-American. He was forced out as foreign minister, clearly with Khomeini's approval.

His political revenge came two months later when he was elected president. But as president too, his efforts were confounded time and again by the Islamic militants holding the embassy.

Black Friday. In 1978, they say, the Shah's army killed 4,000 people in demonstrations in Tehran. Bani-Sadr commemorates the second anniversary at Martyr's Square, trying to gain popular support.

JOSEPH D. STAFFORD · KATHLEEN F. STAFFOR

MERCi 🍁
ₒₐₙₐᵈ

HENRY LEE SCHATZ

In Canada, Prime Minister Joe Clark faced long odds for reelection against Pierre Trudeau. In Iran, another office seeker, Finance Minister Bani-Sadr had just overwhelmed Prime Minister Ghotbzadeh in the presidential election. Something happened to affect both their administrations on . . .

DAY 86

When last seen November 4, Mark Lijek was casually strolling away from Fort Apache as fast as he could manage. He was the consular officer who had managed to slip out the back way.

The man he had been helping, Kim King, had melted into the city. He managed to borrow air fare and left for home November 9. Lijek had walked about four blocks with him, then split. The fugitives agreed to meet the next day at the British Embassy. That plan was scrubbed when street demonstrators overran that legation temporarily. Lijek made his way to an abandoned bungalow. He was not alone.

Somehow, his wife, Cora, a secretary at the embassy, had gotten out, too, and rejoined him. So had Joseph Stafford, aged twenty-nine, a consular officer from Crossville, Tennessee, and his twenty-eight year-old wife, Kathleen; and a secretary Anders, who had gone out the door with them. How they managed was not disclosed, but there they were in a hostile town with their freedom their only possession.

Four days after the takeover, they contacted the Canadian Embassy. Canadian Ambassador Ken Taylor, aged fifty-five, an easygoing type, was only too happy to help. They showed up at the embassy on November 10 and were hidden away in homes of the Canadians. Two weeks later they were joined by a sixth American, Henry Lee Schatz, aged thirty-one, agricultural attache from Post Falls, Idaho. He had been staying with friends.

Washington knew they were out and informed their families, but admonished them to say nothing. But how to get them out of Iran?

Buying food was no problem. With the shortages in the city, people were moving in with others and toting home extra groceries was nothing out of the ordinary. The Americans laid low, amusing themselves with games of Scrabble and listening to broadcasts about developments surrounding their less fortunate colleagues. They played so much Scrabble, Anders said, "Some of us could identify the letter on the

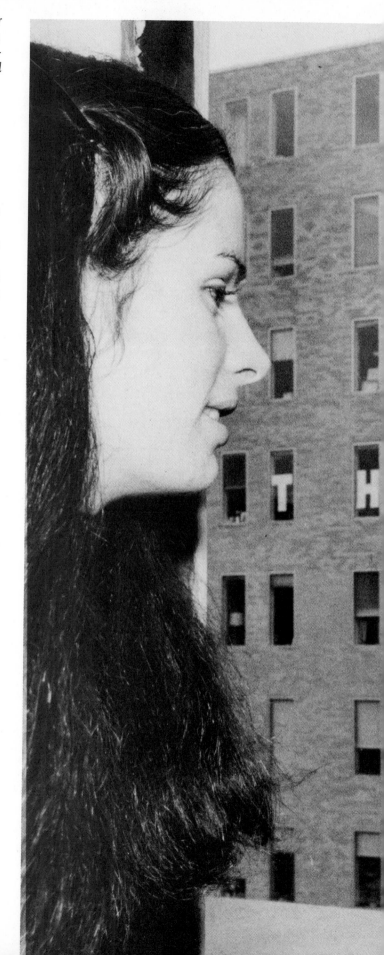

Grateful. Washingtonians expressed their gratitude to Canada for the rescue of six American diplomats with window signs across from the Canadian Embassy.

front by the shape of the grain on the back of the tile."

"I'd nominate any of them for the world Scrabble championship," Taylor said. "They are also probably the six best-read foreign service officers."

Taylor realized the concealment couldn't go on indefinitely. He spent a lot of time at the Foreign Ministry hobnobbing with the Iranians and quietly learning what documents the Americans would need to slip out of the country. He sent his own personnel on unneeded trips just to learn exit procedures. In Canada, a special secret Cabinet meeting agreed to issue Canadian passports to the Americans under false names. The CIA provided bogus Iranian stamps.

On January 19, an anonymous caller phoned the Taylor's home asking for the Staffords. Taylor's wife , Patricia, feigned ignorance, but the caller said he knew the Staffords were there. So did some news agencies, but had kept the secret. Taylor decided he had to move quickly. He reduced his staff to a skeleton political officer, communications aide, secretary and guard. On January 28, he posted a note on the door of the embassy saying it was closed. Then they all went to the airport, passed through immigration and took a plane for Frankfurt.

Back home, they appeared briefly at a State Department news conference. "I'm still walking on air," said Stafford, "but the State Department said they'd rather we didn't talk too much." His father, a vice president of the Occidental Petroleum Company, had known his son was hiding out somewhere in Tehran, "But I didn't ask where."

The escapees smiled like fat cats for the photographers, then, like diplomats, dropped from the public eye.

The Canadian-U.S. border never seemed a better mark of good will. "Thank You, Canada," proclaimed a huge billboard in Detroit across from Windsor, Ontario. Flora Macdonald, Canada's foreign minister, received early Valentine messages saying, "I love you." President Carter phoned Joe Clark to thank him for "a tremendous exhibition of friendship and support and political courage."

One of the militants at the U.S. Embassy exclaimed: "That's illegal!"

He provided one of the few last laughs of an otherwise long winter.

Americans respond. Canadian Embassy employees in Washington are inundated in thank you letters from across the United States.

11

The serious, bespectacled man visited the frail servant of Allah in the hospital to receive his blessing as president. For the Iranians it was the first time in 2,500 years they had not been ruled by a monarch. For the Americans at the embassy it was...

DAY 96

Abolhassan Bani-Sadr, a 46-year-old economist and son of an ayatollah, had been dropped as foreign minister in December for criticizing the militants holding the hostages. As he took office with Khomeini's personal acknowledgement February 7, he spoke against them once again.

They were "rebels against the government," he declared.

Who they were was not that clear. They were shadows, unnamed, unknown soldiers of an undetermined cause. They were referred to as students, and some apparently were. Some were believed to be radicals who had received training from the Palestine Liberation Organization of Yassir Arafat. Washington believed their primary goal was to make trouble for the United States rather than extort the return of the Shah. But no one could say with certainty whose finger was on the trigger inside the compound nor at what the gun was aimed.

The trouble, said President Carter, was "there's nobody there with whom we can get in touch."

With Bani-Sadr in office, there was at least someone now with constituted authority. And he at last was willing to discuss the matter. He outlined areas for negotiation in a telephone interview with Newsweek magazine.

"I have always said that something must change between us and the Americans. And this change can only come from the American side. The United States must take the initiative on three different points if it wants to change the political climate. It must condemn its past policy in Iran. It must promise it will not obstruct the pursuit of the Shah, his entourage and other criminals for their financial corruption, their treason and their other crimes. If these three conditions are met, the climate will change. And we can start over in a new political and psychological climate.

"The reality is that we want to extradite the Shah, and the Americans want the hostages freed. What we need to find is the point at which these two curves intersect. I explained all this to the Imam, and he agreed. I think that the United States is in a position to make the extradition of the Shah possible."

Did he think the United States would agree?

"Ask Mr. Carter."

For his part, Mr. Carter said: "I will not do anything to violate the principles of our country. And I will not do anything to violate our obligations to Iran. I'm more optimistic now than I was a few weeks ago."

The question of the Shah's wealth was a sample demonstration that the two nations were not speaking the same language. The Iranians thought the president of the United States could exert his will at the dial of a telephone. They had obviously never tried to cash a check at an out-of-town bank in America.

Even if the president had the authority to obtain any Pahlavi family money in the United States, which he didn't, it was doubtful whether he or anyone else would know where to start. Assuming the Shah had large holdings in U.S. institutions, and assuming these had not been moved to closed accounts in Switzerland, records showed a myriad of secret corporations and fictitious names associated with family members. Several relatives of the Shah had holdings in the United States but not under their own names. Property worth more than $1.5 million in Santa Barbara, California, was owned by the Shah's sister, Princess Shams. But the owner was listed as Rymon J. Rayem Jr.

The Shah's half-sister, Fatemah Pahlavi, owned a fortress-like home in Santa Barbara worth several million dollars. The owner was recorded as the Lambourne Corp. which was located in the Netherlands Antilles. Two town houses in New York belonging to the Shah's twin sister, Princess Ashraf, had been transferred to two other Netherlands Antilles corporations. Obviously the Shah's finances were Byzantine, whatever else they were.

•   •   •

Diplomacy does not happen live on TV. And it does not happen overnight. But its ancient if fusty practices were slowly being put to work. At the United Nations Kurt Waldheim was trying to form a commission to investigate Iran's grievances.

"An appropriate commission with a carefully defined purpose would be a step toward resolution of this crisis," Carter said. To keep the door ajar, the United States decided not to invoke sanctions against trade with Iran. Three French lawyers who handled Iran's financial legal matters had been in touch with Washington. Complicating matters were attempts by the Iranians to extradite the Shah from Panama, The exiled emperor had taken up residence on the tiny resort island of Contadora sixty miles off the Panamanian coast.

Dilemma. For President Jimmy Carter there were no answers to the hostage problem.

Former Panamanian president Omar Torrijos, who had become a beer-drinking buddy of Carter aide Hamilton Jordan during the Canal negotiations, apparently owed the United States one and volunteered to take a hot potato off America's hands.

Even with Bani-Sadr in office, it was not clear who was in charge. Iranian sources said no decision could be made in any case until a parliament was elected in March. Infighting in Tehran continued to blur lines of authority. The militants managed to have National Guidance Minister Nasser Minachi arrested, claiming he was a CIA collaborator. Bani-Sadr promptly released him. Then he cut off the militants' uncensored access to Iranian TV and radio.

Incredibly, the United States could still dial directly into the compound and talk to the militants. But the conversations were limited to mail privileges and such, not grand matters of diplomacy.

The American presidential election was obviously a sword that cut both ways. The Iranians had not spent centuries haggling in bazaars for nothing. The hostage issue would obviously play a part in the campaign, and Carter might be susceptible to Iranian pressure to secure American votes.

Carter, on the other hand, "has to make absolutely certain that it will not look like he has given in too much," said a United Nations diplomat. "We all know that there is a man named Kennedy looking over his shoulder." And a man named Ronald Reagan and a man named John Anderson a little to the rear.

"I am willing to work with Iran in any way, hopefully so that neither side will have to lose face," said the president who had been running for office by staying in it almost exclusively. This became known as Carter's Rose Garden Strategy. However, roses, as is commonly known, have thorns.

.   .   .

On Contadora, the ailing Shah enjoyed the sun but thought the climate too hot and humid. He occasionally walked Lemon, the Great Dane, and even talked with newsmen on his patio. "We were so shocked by this question of the hostages that I even volunteered to leave the New York hospital to help solve the problem," he said.

His wife water skied under the watchful eyes of twenty-five guards uniformed in T-shirts and baseball caps and carrying machine guns. She toughed it out in the kitchen with services of only a cook, butler and maid.

"She is running the house like any other housewife, not like an empress," said their host, former Panamanian Ambassador to the U.S., Gabriel Lewis Galindo.

As for the Shah, King of Kings, his empire was now down to an island, ten acres small.

Exile. With the Americans still hostage, the former Shah and his wife search for haven, land here on Contadora Island, Panama.

Not quite Paradise. The Shah and a dog that is part of his security team jog along the beach at Paradise Island, the Bahamas.

Asylum. In his search for asylum, the Shah and his family even tried the Bahamas.

CHAPTER 12

America goes wild as its hockey team beats Russia and wins a gold medal at the Winter Olympics at Lake Placid to go with skater Eric Heiden's five. Dan Rather signs to replace Walter Cronkite at CBS for $8,000,000. In Tehran it is...

DAY 100

A French newspaper quotes Bani-Sadr as saying Iran will no longer insist on the return of the Shah in exchange for the hostages.

And on...

DAY 105

...Bani-Sadr tells a Greek television newsman the hostages might not be released until the United States undertakes its obligations, one of which is the return of the Shah.

Which newspaper do you read?

The students relent. The guards at the American Embassy carry in bags of Christmas packages for the hostages inside. They are checked first for contraband. ▷

The postman doesn't ring twice. Armed Iranians had the added chore of delivering the thousands of cards and letters to the hostages in the embassy. ▷

Tattered emblem. Even the American flag over the closed U.S. consulate in Tabriz, Iran, was not safe from the mob's wrath. ▲

Tempers flare again. With the abortive rescue attempt came a new reinforcement of guards at the embassy and more posters. ◄

The Ayatollah's son. Seyed Ahmad Khomeini, yet another of the role players in the hostage drama, carries his father's orders to the militant students. ◄

Reagan trounces George Bush and everyone else in New Hampshire's kickoff primary as the campaign gets down to voting time. Carter wins substantially over Kennedy. A U.N. commission has been in Tehran three days on . . .

DAY 115

There is an old joke: what is the difference between a diplomat and a lady? Answer: if she says 'no', she means 'maybe', if she says 'maybe', she means 'yes', if she says 'yes', she's no lady. If a diplomat says yes, he means 'maybe', if he says 'maybe' he means 'no', if he says 'no', he's no diplomat.

The U.N. mission to Tehran was no joke, but then . . .

Secretary-General Kurt Waldheim had chosen a panel of four men with impeccable credentials. They were:

Co-Chairman Andres Aguilar Mawdsley, aged fifty, Algeria's chief delegate to the United Nations, and former government official.

Adib Daoudy, aged fifty-six, Syrian diplomat, an Alawite, a Moslem sect related to the Shiites and a man who said the hostage seizure "has harmed everybody, including Iran and Islam."

Hector Wilfred Jayawardene, sixty-three, a lawyer and brother of Sri Lanka President Junius Richard Jayaardene.

Louis-Edmond Pettiti, aged sixty-five, a French attorney who had once headed a group that investigated charges of torture by SAVAK and knew Bani-Sadr.

Just what the commission was committed to do was clear to no one. Bani-Sadr said it would investigate "the crimes of the ex-Shah and American intervention in Iran."

Waldheim said the panel would "hear Iran's grievances and speak to each of the hostages."

Secretary of State Vance said the commission would not be sitting as a court nor reach a verdict. It was to hear grievances of both sides, but "under no circumstances" was it to interrogate the captive Americans.

Everything was in the eye of the beholder.

The panel waited several hours in Geneva airport for the signal to leave. Then they were recalled for last minute clarifications behind the scene. Finally on February 23, they reached Tehran. This was Day 112.

The following is a chronology of seventeen days that did not shake the world:

February 24: The commission meets with Bani-Sadr in a session that is described as "extremely constructive." But Iranian officials insist the panel's mission is not tied to the release of the hostages.

February 25: The commission hears testimony from Iranian jurists on alleged human rights violations.

February 26: The Revolutionary Council, having thrown Western journalists out of the country six weeks before for "slanting" the news, decides to let them back in.

February 27: Ghotbzadeh and the commission talk about meeting with the hostages.

February 28: Tehran radio says the militants have agreed to let the commission talk to the captives.

March 4: The militants say the commission may not meet with the hostages. Khomeini overrules them. Bani-Sadr says the final decision is up to the Revolutionary Council.

March 5: Ghotbzadeh berates the militants as "Communists and Zionists" for refusing the commission.

March 6: The militants switch horses. They ask the council to take over the hostages and "deal with them in anyway it seems appropriate." This is regarded as a breakthrough. The commission had been packing to leave Iran. They decide to stay.

March 7: The government says even if it takes control of the hostages their fate will be left to the new parliament, still to be elected.

March 8: The militants say they will surrender the hostages that afternoon. Then they learn Ghotbzadeh has been chosen the official to receive them. They threaten to back out of the agreement. Crowds in the street shout their support of the militants.

March 9: Ghotbzadeh gives an ultimatum: turn the hostages over within twenty-four hours or let the commissioner visit them. The militants say they will do so only if the foreign minister steps aside as the receiver of the Americans.

March 10: Khomeini, too, switches fields. The commission cannot see the hostages. The Revolutionary Council switches with him. It drops its demand to take custody of the hostages. White House Press Secretary Jody Powell says events have taken "a very serious turn."

Many turns.

March 11: Bani-Sadr tells the French newspaper Le Monde that the militants are influenced by pro-Soviet groups. The commission, its patience if not its laundry exhausted, gives up and flies home.

March 12: Vance meets with the commission back in New York. He says "the door is still open."

A revolving door, it seemed.

Outside looking in. An Iranian woman looks through the chained gate of the embassy for a glimpse of the Americans inside.

14

Time had become their prison. Minutes became hours, hours days, days weeks over and over. The leaves had gone, the snows had come and now buds were returning. Time and the weeks had become months, in fact . . .

MONTH 6

Another holy day, Christian this time, had come to Tehran. It was April, Day 155, Easter Sunday.

Three American clergymen had come to the embassy from America to give services. They were Jack Bremer of Lawrence, Kansas, and Nelson Thompson of Kansas City, Missouri, Methodists, and the Rev. Darell Rupiper, a Catholic priest from Omaha.

A militant known as Mary met them at the gate at 2 P.M. She warned the clergymen not to discuss politics. Then they ate a turkey lunch. At 4 P.M. they were blindfolded and driven to the compound library.

"We hugged three male hostages, and shed some tears," said Thompson. In groups of two to four, hostages came for services, thirty-one in all. Ahern, Daugherty and Kalp, the alleged spies, were still absent as they had been at Christmas. So was Michael Metrinko, the Persian-speaking former Peace Corpsman. He was reportedly in solitary confinement for having tried to escape.

One of the hostages told of having seen a dove fly to his windowsill. He and his roommates said it was a message of hope, a dove in the greening of spring. "We cried when we heard that story," Thompson said.

"Hang on," said Barry Rosen in a message to his wife. "Don't worry."

"We need more than some prayers," said Robert Ode, the retired foreign service officer. "We need action. We need to get out of here, that's what we need."

Ann Swift and Kathryn Koob, the two women, said they had become roommates and felt "like sisters." The food was good and they could sleep whenever they felt like it, stay up to 2 in the morning, sleep until 11.

During the services, the militants provided a spread of Easter eggs, cakes and fruit. When the hostages left, they took the leftovers with them back to wherever it was they measured their time.

Rosalynn Carter, campaigning for her husband in

Cutting the ties. A State Department employee in Washington has just delivered a note to the Iranian Embassy ordering all its personnel to leave the country.

College Drop Outs. Iranians who were taking military courses at Charleston's Citadel are ordered home with other Iranian personnel.

Getting out. An Iranian couple waits for a flight home at Washington's Dulles Airport following the closing of their embassy. ▷

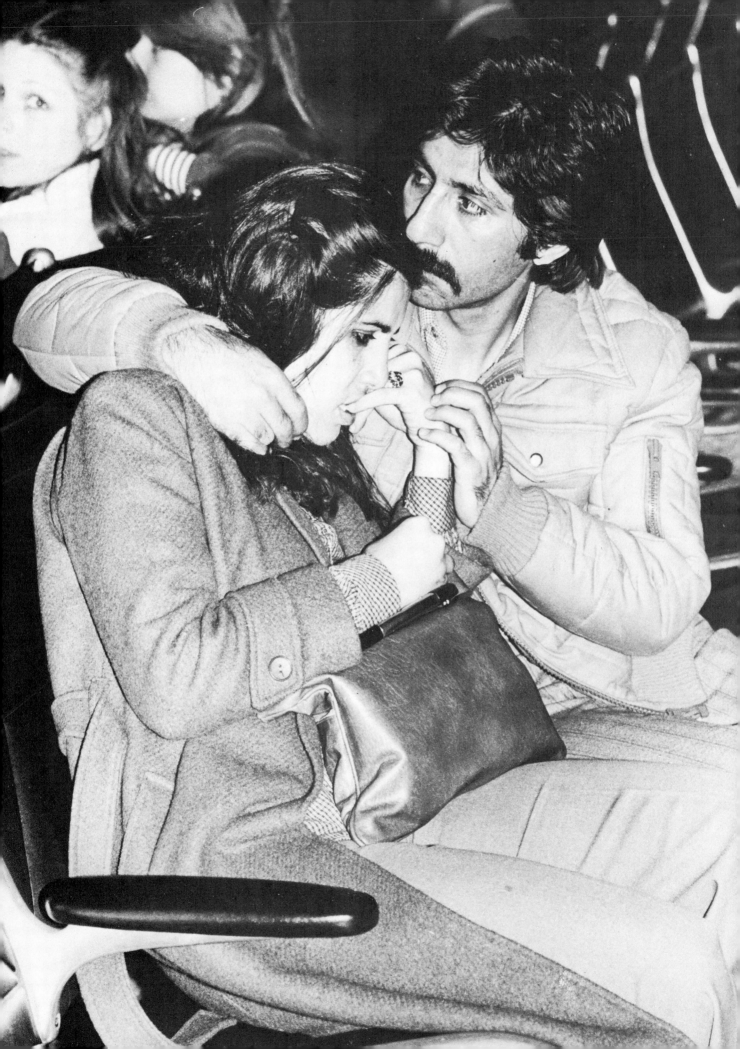

Pennsylvania, had heard Metrinko has missed the services. She stopped her tour to visit his parents in Olyphant, Pennsylvania, to present them with an Easter egg from her daughter Amy.

• • •

One of the hostages, William Keough, the huge school principal, had a daughter at college in Vermont. Allyssa Keough, aged eighteen, had been critical of Carter's handling of the crisis. When an Iranian schoolmate was expelled back to his home, she gave him a farewell hug.

"It's not fair. They are as innocent as the hostages are," she said.

In all, the United States was to interview 59,577 Iranian students in the country. About 10,000 failed to report. Of them, 2,638 requested asylum; 7,771 were found deportable and 681 were actually sent out of the country, 144 having to be bodily escorted to a plane. The others left quietly.

There remained in the United States some 250,000 people of Iranian origins. And thirty-five diplomats.

• • •

For whatever reason, the United States had foreborne to play tit-for-tat with the Iranian consular officials by seizing them. Undoubtedly, any judge in the country would have freed them the next day. It was, after all, a nation of laws.

It was also a world of laws. In accordance with them, the day after Easter, Carter broke diplomatic relations with Iran. Some Americans were surprised it had not already been done long ago. Others wondered why it took so long. In addition, Carter finally invoked sanctions. He embargoed all shipments to Iran from the United States except food and medicine.

That same day, Ali Agah, the Iranian Charge D'affaires in Washington, was summoned to the State Department. He arrived shortly after lunch with an aide, Mohammed Lavassani. They were scheduled to meet with Deputy Secretary of State Warren Christopher. Lavassani was talking with Henry Precht, chief of the Iran desk while they waited. Lavassani observed that his government was protecting the hostages.

Precht had had enough.

"Bullshit!" he snapped.

The two Iranians stomped off to the elevator. Precht tried to block their way. Christopher hadn't yet delivered a formal notification of the rupture of relations. Agah said he could deliver it to his embassy.

"We will not take it any longer to have any of my brothers insulted," the irate Iranian shouted to reporters.

Nonetheless, he and his fellow diplomats in five consu-

Protective custody. District of Columbia police cordon off the Iranian Embassy to protect the diplomats who were ordered to leave.

lates across the country were given thirty-six hours to leave the United States.

In Tehran, Khomeini exulted at the news. He said it meant that the United States had given up hope of influencing affairs in Iran. Bani-Sadr said: "I tell the nation it is a war."

Not quite. But it wasn't peace.

.   .   .

It was not quite war, either, on the Iran-Iraq border. But it was not peace. Near the border town of Bavaeissi, on April 9, Iran had recalled its diplomats in Baghdad. Both sides accused the other of acting for U.S. "imperialists."

.   .   .

Having taken the step himself, Carter tried to get America's NATO allies to embargo Iran as well. They were reluctant. The British pointed out that sanctions had done little harm to Rhodesia. Italy had $3 billion worth of construction contracts in Iran and 1,800 of her workers. Germany did not want to jeopardize its $7 billion-a-year trade with the Soviet Union. Japan imported thirteen percent of its oil from Iran—620,000 barrels a day.

On April 10, the nine nations of the European Common Market issued a "demand" that Iran release the hostages. But they stopped short of sanctions. Twelve days later, they announced they would reduce their diplomatic staffs in Tehran and impose sanctions if no "decisive progress" was made within a month.

Washington was not pleased with the French, who had argued against sanctions at a Common Market meeting in Lisbon. It did not help, either, when France's roving ambassador, Michel Poniatowski, was quoted in a West German magazine as saying Carter was "an imbecile."

A Carter aide fumed. "The French have never done a goddamn thing for us. They turned belly up in World War I, and we saved their asses. They turned belly up in World War II, and we saved their asses again. Now they turn their goddamn Gallic noses up at us like we're a bunch of heathens."

On April 23, however, Japan and Canada approved political and economic sanctions against Iran.

.   .   .

Let nations struggle, Barbara Timm was a mother. And she wanted to see her son, Sgt. Kevin Hermening, a hostage, and see that her boy was being taken care of.

On April 20, Day 170, Mrs. Timm walked where Carters and Vances had not trod and spent forty-five minutes with her baby. She said they were taking care of him just fine.

.   .   .

The day Mrs. Timm left the United States, Carter said he had heard Khomeini would not release the hostages until after the U.S. presidential election. That would be November 4, a year to the day after their seizure, Day 365.

.   .   .

The Easter visit had provided the best photographs so far of the hostages. Many of the men were growing beards. Donald Hohman had looked decidedly angry. Kathryn Koob, the smiling onetime church worker, wore a cross around her neck.

As Carter tightened the screws, the militants began showing TV film of purported espionage equipment in the embassy. Sgt. Joe Subic was shown lifting up a carpet to reveal wires he said were CIA antennae to monitor Iranian communications.

Gumbleton, the Detroit bishop who had visited the embassy at Christmas, was asked about it. He said Subic had whispered to him: "This whole thing is staged."

Even from behind the walls, there was gossip.

.   .   .

As the end of April neared, the carrier Constellation with six escort craft was on her way to join the American fleet in the Indian Ocean off Iran. This would bring United States strength there to thirty-four vessels.

If the United States tried "even the smallest" military action against Iran, said the militants, they would burn the embassy and kill the hostages. Even the smallest military action. Burn. Then kill.

Reunion. One of the hostages, Kevin Hermening, is allowed a brief visit with his mother, Barbara Timm, who flew to Tehran to see him.

HERMITAGE, PENNSYLVANIA

Each day at 8:00 A.M., fair weather or foul, an American flag was raised in Hillcrest Memorial Park in the rural northwestern Pennsylvania town of Hermitage to mark another day of captivity for the fifty-two American hostages. The idea originated with Hillcrest's owner, Tom Flynn.

Some of the banners grew tattered and frayed. Others snapped out stiffly in the raw autumn wind—their stars intact and their bars still bright red. They bore quiet testimony to the deep concern felt by individual Americans for their fellow citizens held captive half a world away.

The flags were all donated by private citizens. Many covered the caskets of veterans who died for their country at places like Anzio Beach, Casablanca, Vietnam and in the trenches of France during World War I.

Note after touching note arrived at Hillcrest Memorial Park, after the flags started flying high in February 1980. Some writers told stories about the husbands, fathers and brothers for whom the accompanying flags were dedicated. Others included poetry. Most said they prayed for the hostages.

"I know that this flag was never part of a historic event. It is just an average flag from an average town. But I feel that this simple flag represents the silent majority of American people," said a note enclosed with a flag from Victoria Gibbons of Olmstead Falls, Ohio.

A vigil flame also burned at the site for hostage Michael Metrinko. His parents, Harry and Alice Metrinko, live in Olyphant, near Scranton, across the state from Hermitage. They have been involved in all of the cemetery's observances involving the hostages.

On February 11, 1979, the one hundredth day of captivity, one hundred flags were raised. The Metrinkos journeyed to Hermitage to light the vigil flame.

"I still get shivers when I think about it," recalled Mrs. Catherine Mack, Hillcrest's public relations manager. "People walked out of the chapel holding candles and burst into 'God Bless America' when Harry lit the flame."

In March, Tom Flynn, Catherine Mack and five others began what turned out to be a 670-mile trek to show their support for the hostages. In relays, the walkers trudged across rural, mountainous central Pennsylvania to the Metrinko home in Olyphant. Along the way, they got the worldwide news coverage and the support they sought. "All along that walk, the one thing we found was that people cared," said Mrs. Mack.

CHAPTER 15

Fidel Castro lifted the gates and a sealift brought thousands of Cubans across the straits to Florida. Eastern Airlines would put you up in Miami, $499 for eight days and seven nights. Gay Talese wrote a book about sex in America. Sevie Ballesteros won the Masters. Aboard the U.S. carrier Nimitz in the Arabian Sea it was dawn, April 24 . . .

DAY 173

George Holmes Jr., a Marine corporal, had packed up his personal gear, threw in his last paycheck and mailed it all home to his family in Pine Bluff, Arkansas. He said he wouldn't be needing it for a while.

Rosalynn Carter was in Austin campaigning for her White House-bound husband.

In Washington, a very select few showed up early for work.

On the Carrier Nimitz, eight big helicopters coughed in the predawn and their six dragon fly rotos began swooping around the flight deck.

Six C-130 Hercules transports took off from an undisclosed airfield in Egypt.

All had a rendezvous this spring day.

George Holmes was member of an elite, secret force of three hundred men from all the services known as Operation Blue Light. Among themselves they were "Charlie's Angels," named after their leader, Col. Charles A. Beckwith, a fifty-one-year-old Georgian and unsung hero of the Vietnam War. Beckwith was so secret, "even his middle name is classified," said a newsman who had known him. So were his men. They were picked because "they are highly intelligent, in good physical condition and can keep their mouths shut."

For months they had been practicing in the deserts of the Southwest for a mission in their specialty, commando rescue operations. They were organized in 1977 after the German and Israeli rescue raids at Mogadishu and Entebbe.

They were stationed at Fort Bragg, North Carolina, behind a fourteen-foot fence in a compound that was originally the base prison. They trained at such things as bursting into a darkened room with special goggles and infra-red gear and blasting tight groups of holes with Uzi machine guns in photographs pinned on the wall. One newspaper said a team of them had been flown into Iran right after the hostages were seized but flown out again when President Carter decided force was out. Now he had decided force was back in.

•   •   •

Plans for military contingencies had begun November 9, only five days after the embassy was seized. At Carter's order, Brzezinski sat down with Defense Secretary Harold Brown, Air Force Gen. David Jones, chairman of the Joint Chiefs of Staff, and Vice President Walter Mondale. They met for ten days. Some of the options discussed included the Blue Lights. Thus they began training, although their actual use was considered remote. Carter had opted for the high road of diplomacy and economic pressure.

After six months, however, the hostages were still hostages. By the end of March, the Carter Administration felt political stability in Iran was deteriorating. When, on April 7, Khomeini ruled that the hostages must remain in the hands of the militants, Carter believed he had to act.

He convened the National Security Council April 11 and, in a little more than an hour, decided to act.

The plan needed luck and timing. It certainly had had planning.

•   •   •

Seven times the Blue Lights had held rehearsals, some at night. Col. Beckwith much preferred the dark.

Reportedly, American agents had been infiltrating into Iran, some disguised as European businessmen.

Eight 25-ton Sikorsky RH-53 helicopters, called Sea Stallions, had long been aboard the Nimitz. They were designed as mine sweepers, but much of their electronic gear was removed to increase their range: 800 miles. The best mechanics the Navy could muster were aboard the Nimitz as well as some technicians from the manufacturer. But the armed services had had trouble in keeping their best men. One Navy report had listed the "mission capable" rating of the Sea Stallion at less than fifty per cent. But the Navy was to maintain this rating was for the fully loaded mine sweeper version, not the stripped down chopper. The crews carefully tended their big birds and sent them out on repeated test flights. (None, however, lasted more than three-and-a-half hours. The mission called for eight.)

"The helicopter detachment aboard the Nimitz had all the people and technical skills the on-scene commanders said they needed, in contrast to the shortages which are standard elsewhere in the Navy," said Adm. Thomas Hayward, Chief of Naval Operations.

Recently the Nimitz had stepped up Sea Stallion takeoffs to avert any suspicion that a mass takeoff was anything but routine. C-130s did the same in Egypt. Just practice. One morning it was for real, and the four-engine prop planes

The day after at Desert One and America's armed might lay strewn across the desert like parched camels.

113

headed down the Red Sea, destination: Iran.

They stopped for fuel somewhere on the west coast of the Persian Gulf, possibly Oman. There they rendezvoused with the helicopters. On board were ninety Blue Lights and ninety airmen. Flying low to avoid radar, they headed for a spot designated Desert One, a moonscape salt pan ringed by mountains 250 miles southeast of Tehran. An earlier C-130 had landed there, reportedly, to test if the terrain could support the big planes. It could. The plan was based on the premise that Iranian radar would be expecting a rescue attempt to come from the west, not the east.

The night before, five of the eight helicopters had been accidentally doused with a mixture of foam and sea water when a sailor set off a fire-fighting system by mistake. The aircraft were scrubbed and checked out and deemed operational. After all, they were meant to operate in a salt water environment.

As the choppers whirred in over land, well along on their 530-mile journey, a red warning light blinked in one of them. It indicated one of the aluminum rotors had cracked. The pilot set the craft down. An indicator on the hub also showed trouble. The crew picked up classified equipment and transferred to another chopper. They left the aircraft intact for fear of alerting the Iranians by blowing it up.

Now there were seven.

There were thunderstorms off to the west. Apparently the bad weather kicked up a sandstorm. The pilots suddenly found themselves "flying in a milk bowl, a darkened milk bowl at that." At that point a helicopter lost its gyroscope, essential for blind flying at night. A flak jacket and a duffel bag had apparently been left against a cooling vent, causing a motor to burn out. The pilot didn't dare to climb out of the storm for fear of being picked up by radar. He turned back to the Nimitz.

Then there were six.

They fought through the storm for three hours. The 201-pound sand screens had been removed from each helicopter to increase lift capacity by three percent. Beckwith was already on the ground waiting for the birds. He is an hour behind schedule already "and Beckwith gets paranoid because he likes darkness," he said later. One of the reasons the mission had to go in the spring was to avoid the long twilights of summer. Also, in that season the air is lighter, reducing the helicopter's lift. No, it had to be now or never.

At 12:50 A.M. April 25, the helicopters began arriving. The last got in at 1:40.

Beckwith started inspecting his small squadron. "When I came up on, I think the third chopper in line, one of the pilots climbed out and told me that one of the helicopters was not flyable." A backup hydraulic system had failed be-

In the wreckage lay eight Americans dead in a raid that failed. Did the hostages know? The world did, and President Carter and his nation were humiliated.

115

cause a nut had cracked, draining the system and burning out a pump. It would not be safe to fly with only one system.

Now there were five.

. . .

Oddly, the Iranians knew about Desert One, a spot called Posht-i-Badam. Then even had a map of it. It had been found when militiamen arrested Mahmoud Jaafarian, a Shah counterinsurgency expert who had been in on the CIA's construction of the site as a possible emergency strip. Jaafarian had been trying to burn the map when he was arrested. He was later executed. The Iranians figured the Americans would certainly not use the site now that the secret was out.

But there was other traffic that night.

A Mercedes bus bound from Tehran to Tabas, about 100 miles away, came driving across the desert. It headed right for the landing zone where the transports had just finished unloading the Blue Lights. The soldiers stopped the bus. One of the passengers said he thought at first the men were bandits. But they had American flags on their shoulders. The men disabled the bus by shooting at its engine block.

"A couple of them spoke Persian," the passenger said later. "They told us to get off the bus and raise our hands. They said no one would be hurt unless we tried something funny." The driver screamed. "They hit him on the head with a rifle butt. They tied his hands behind his back. They told us all to lie down on the ground."

Officers on motorcycles rushed to have a conference. They were in direct radio contact with Washington by satellite. It was decided to fly them out on one of the C-130s. "They were going to have a nice long trip," an American said.

Then a tank truck came rumbling down the road that ran right through the landing zone. Soldiers fired at its headlights. The truck burst into flames. The driver scurried out and ran into a pickup truck that had been following behind. The pickup sped into the night. What to do now?

Beckwith conferred with Washington and the overall mission commander, Army Maj. Gen. James Vaught. It was decided not to scrub the mission. The trucks had probably been carrying smugglers. The last place they would want to be seen was a police station.

But there was a even graver question. The plan called for cancellation of the rescue if only five helicopters were left. That left no contingency for further failure. If something happened to another chopper, some people would have to be left behind. The Sea Stallions could carry thirty-seven people. There were ninety commandos and fifty-three hostages.

116

Army Col. Charles Beckwith

"My God, I'm going to fail," Beckwith thought.

He conferred with Air Force Col. James Kyle, the commander on the ground. "Jim, let's confirm this (the hydraulic failure) because I want to make sure." Kyle checked and confirmed it. "Sir," said Beckwith, "my recommendation is that we abort."

Kyle: "Would you consider taking five and going ahead? Think about it before answering me. Really, you're the guy who's got to shoulder this, Charlie."

Beckwith: "I know."

Beckwith thought for a few seconds, then said: "There's just no way."

In Washington, Gen. Jones, Brown and Vaught agreed. Scrub, they advised Carter. Yes, said Carter. It was just after five o'clock in Washington. The White House told the press corps there would be no more news for the day. Most of the reporters left.

It was 2:10 A.M. on the desert. The Blue Lights began transferring their gear out of the helicopters back to the C-130s. The pilot of one of the Sea Stallions nudged his craft about twenty feet in the air to go around a transport to a tanker plane on the other side. As he banked in the darkness, a rotor slashed into the transport just aft of the crew compartment.

Suddenly Posht-i-Badam burst into flame. The fireball was visible for miles. Around the world, in fact.

FLAG—FAMILY LIAISON ACTION GROUP, INC.

It began as a self-help group, an organization run by and for hostage families.

Today, the Family Liaison Action Group Inc., known as FLAG, is a full-fledged corporation with its own offices in downtown Washington, a board of directors, a fairly regular newsletter and a respectable bank account. The organization has raised more than $150,000 from private and corporate donors.

"The bottom line is that having this organization creates the emotional bond that all families share with each other," said Louisa Kennedy, who helped found the organization in March 1980, when the families realized the hostage crisis might not be resolved for months.

"We're the only people who can understand the real meaning of being a hostage family," Mrs. Kennedy said. "And it's easier to keep your chin up when you're surrounded by friends."

FLAG's purpose was to help the families of the fifty-two Americans held captive in Iran, to keep them informed of late developments, to help them deal with the news media, to answer their questions and keep them abreast of hostage ceremonies and events taking place around the country.

"Basically, we're like a public relations firm," said Mrs. Kennedy, whose husband, Moorhead C. Kennedy, was one of the hostages. "We're a booking agency. We're spokesman for the families. We know their overall sentiment, worry, concern."

FLAG's major activity in December 1980 was to encourage groups to send Christmas cards in the name of the hostages to various institutions in their community, such as homes for the elderly or children.

When a French group offered to send the captives fifty-two Christmas trees, FLAG members suggested that instead, one tree be sent to Paris for a ceremony honoring the four American hostages who once lived in France.

The office received as many as eighty calls a day from civic groups and institutions that wanted to do something for the hostages or their families.

FLAG, which was originally situated in the State Department, moved a few blocks away to a suite of offices donated by a private law firm. Its furniture was donated by a furniture store, and it is decorated with donated plants and television sets. The building management pays the electric bill.

FLAG's new, private office offers hostage families members a place to go for private counseling or calls to other families.

She raised the FLAG. Louisa Kennedy, wife of hostage Moorhead Kennedy Jr., Islamic law scholar and economic specialist, kept her cool as spokeswoman for the Family Liason Action Group.

117

The rescue effort had been one of Jimmy Carter's best kept secrets. He had not even told his wife, normally his closest confidante.

The decision to abort the mission had left those in the know in the White House in gloom. Carter and Brzezinski were joined by Mondale, Warren Christopher of State, Powell, Jordan and a little later, Brown and Vance.

"At least", said Carter, "there were no casualties, and there was no detection. It could have been worse." It was 6:21 P.M. local time. At that moment came word of the crash. The president was stunned. Then came word that eight men had died in the flames. The secret could be kept a secret no longer. The White House group was joined by Adm. Stansfield Turner, head of the CIA, who had been following events at his office. They all moved into the Cabinet Room to ponder what to do. Would the militants carry out their threats to kill the hostages? If so, then what? At 7:30 P.M. came word that the C-130s were airborne with the survivors. The White House group ordered sandwiches. The talk continued.

• • •

The five Air Force crewmen in the C-130 died in the fire as did three Marines on board the helicopter. The pilot of the Sea Stallion was badly burned along with three others. Fearing a chain of explosions, Beckwith ordered the remaining four helicopters abandoned, possibly leaving behind classified documents as well as the plan for rescuing the hostages. The C-130s took off for Egypt, leaving the dead behind. Night once again took over the desert.

• • •

The first White House announcement came at 1 A.M. April 25. It was terse, with few details.

The Associated Press moved a bulletin at 1:22: "WASHINGTON (AP)—The White House announced early Friday that a daring military effort to rescue American hostages held in Tehran was aborted because of "equipment failure." A collision of two U.S. aircraft on the ground in an Iranian desert resulted in the deaths of eight crewmen, the announcement said."

The president was scheduled to elaborate in a telecast at 7 A.M. His wife had been alerted and was flying through the night to be at her husband's side. Aides meanwhile were hurriedly briefing Congressional leaders.

The president was understandably grim when he entered the studio. He had asked for transcripts of President Kennedy's address after the failure of the Bay of Pigs invasion

of Cuba in 1961. There was a similarity in tone.

"It was my decision to attempt the rescue mission," he said. "It was my decision to cancel it when problems developed. The responsibility is fully my own."

That, as he well knew, would not be the last word.

• • •

For obvious reasons, the government did not describe in detail what the rescue attempt had entailed. The plan had called for the helicopters to fly to a mountain area shielded from radar about 100 miles from Tehran. There, nondescript buses and trucks were to carry the assault forces into the city. They were to be aided by American agents already in place and possibly Iranian sympathizers. The men were under orders not to start a fight with Iranian forces but to defend themselves. There was talk that several of the militants in the compound had been "turned."

At first, it was reported the rescue team carried a disabling gas, but this was later denied. They were armed conventionally. It was believed the hostages would have been quickly rounded up, including Laingen, Tomseth and Howland at the Foreign Ministry. The helicopters would land either on the soccer field inside the compound or on rooftops. Then they would lift off, rendezvous with the C-130s and leave Iran. It was said that deaths had been anticipated, including perhaps as many as fifteen of the hostages.

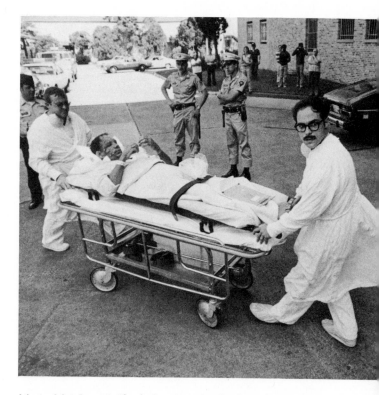

Marine Maj. James J. Shaefer Jr., of Los Angeles, burned in the aborted rescue attempt, is rushed to Brooke Army Medical Center in San Antonio, Texas.

U.S. aircraft were to have been in the air along Iran's borders on call to interdict any movement by Iranian forces.

In his talk, Carter said the plan had "an excellent chance of success. The readiness of our team made it completely practical." Jim Wright, Democratic leader of the House, said the mission had run afoul of "an almost unbelievable chain of bad luck."

For want of a nail, the horse had failed. For want of a horse, a kingdom had fallen. For want of an hydraulic nut in the desert . . .

.   .   .

The Iranians sent a team to the site afterwards. Iranian planes strafed the helicopters, destroying at least two of them. An Iranian soldier was killed and two were wounded during the strafing.

The bodies were bought back to Tehran and displayed in coffins inside the compound. One enraged Iranian opened a coffin and stabbed a body in the head. The skull disintegrated.

An Iranian officer gave his view of the operation. "The planning and the execution were too incompetent to believe. If the mission was scrubbed for the reason stated, then the Americans were lucky that they failed in the first stage. If this was the level of their preparation, the actual raid on Tehran would have been a catastrophe."

It was all of that anyway.

Archbishop Hilarion Capudji talks with Red Cross officials in Zurich, Switzerland, as he stands behind one of the coffins with the remains of the killed American commandos.

RESCUE MISSION
The eight servicemen who died in the helicopter accident during the hostage rescue attempt was the largest number of U.S. servicemen to die in action since the freighter Mayaguez was rescued from Cambodia in 1975.

Five other members of the anti-terrorist strike force known as Operation Blue Light were injured and flown back to a hero's welcome at Kelly Air Force Base in Texas.

But the retreating commandos had no time to recover the bodies of their fallen comrades.

Those killed in the rescue mission were:
—Corporal George Holmes Jr., twenty-two-year-old Marine from Pine Bluff, Arkansas.
—Captain Richard Bakke, thirty-three-year-old Air Force captain from Long Beach, California.
—Marine S/Sgt. Dewey Johnson, twenty-one years old, from Jacksonville, North Carolina.
—Harold Lewis, Air Force captain from Mansfield, Connecticut. He was thirty-five.
—Air Force T/Sgt. Joel Mayo, thirty-four-year-old from Bonifay, Florida.
—Air Force Capt. Lyn McIntosh, thirty-three years old, from Valdosta, Georgia.
—Air Force Capt. Charles McMillan, twenty-eight-year-old, from Corryton, Tennessee.
—Marine Sgt. John Davis Harvey, twenty-one years old, from Roanoke, Virginia.

16

Richard Helms, the former CIA director had been the last U.S. Ambassador to Iran before Sullivan. He said: "The timing is peculiar. You spend so much effort getting your allies to take some other line of approach. And just when you seem to be succeeding, you pull this caper." It was the morning after...

DAY 175

Carter was clearly in trouble, as a leader and as a candidate for re-election.

"I have no right to ask you to be supportive," he told a group of Congressmen, "but if you're inclined to do so, it would be helpful."

He was in a sympathetic position. But the fiasco in the desert raised deep uneasiness in a nation that prided itself on its technology being second to none. Israel, a tiny country, had pulled off a similar operation brilliantly. The most powerful nation on earth, second to Russia in orbiting a satellite, defeated in Vietnam, had stumbled again. And James Earl Carter would bear the brunt.

The European nations, who had finally succumbed to U.S. pressure to curtail dealings with Iran, were fuming. "We went to all this trouble to show solidarity with Carter's position, and then he pulls something like this," said an official of the Common Market. An Israeli official said the raid was "too incompetent to believe." *Le Monde* editorialized: "What should we think of a military apparatus upon which the security of half the world depends and which can't fly two airplanes (to) a stretch of desert before the enemy has even been engaged?"

American political figures rallied 'round the flag. But a high West German leader said: "The incompetence which permeates this administration is incredible."

The issue of competence had been raised before about Carter's government. Now it had been raised anew.

In Iran, Ghotbzadeh termed the raid "an act of war." But he was more moderate in private. He said no harm would come to the hostages if the United States refrained from further raids. As a precaution however, the hostages were scattered to other cities in the country.

· · ·

Mrs. Timm was still in Tehran after the raid. She appeared with Bani-Sadr on television and expressed deep regret and apologies for the U.S. action. Then she broke into tears.

In Reston, Virginia, hostage John Graves' wife Bonnie said: "Eight deaths for what?" Mrs. Laingen wired the White House: "I support you. It's tragic it didn't work. Do not despair. Try again."

At the same time, a West German magazine took pictures of the hostages just before they were dispersed. They showed Richard Queen arm wrestling with Joseph Hall; Ode riding a stationary bicycle; Keough, seemingly slimmer, doing pullups. Keough, the magazine said, was going through a book every thirty-six hours and had rewritten a comic book text in verse. Leland Holland did jigsaw puzzles and was reading through an encyclopedia plus *The Making of the President 1972* by Theodore H. White.

The hostages even had a mascot, a brown and white mongrel.

So some word had filtered out from behind the walls. They were Rip Van Winkles, almost but not quite suspended in time. Had they heard of the rescue effort to bring them back from this timeless prison? No one could say.

A campaigning President Carter wears the Polish eagle while grasping for votes in Philadelphia's Polish section. Elsewhere in the city some other Eagles march towards the Super Bowl.

OTHER HOSTAGE INCIDENTS

Schoolchildren in the Netherlands.

Diplomats in Colombia

Athletes in West Germany.

Americans in Iran.

Hostages in terror. Captives taken in the name of a political cause. Human beings turned into victims because they were in the wrong place at the wrong time.

The Americans who were prisoners of Iranian militants who took over the U.S. Embassy in Tehran on November 4, 1979, were held far longer than any other group of hostages.

They were also different from other hostages because their captivity was sanctioned by a government. "For a government to applaud mob violence and terrorism, for a government actually to support, and in effect, participate in the taking and holding of hostages, is unprecedented in human history," said President Carter, less than a month after the embassy takeover.

Until 1980, the longest siege was in 1977 in the Netherlands. It involved a group of South Moluccans, seeking independence for their homeland, a part of Indonesia that was formerly a Dutch colony.

One band of terrorist Moluccans seized a commuter train; another took over a school about twelve miles away. The hostages at the school included more than one hundred children.

The children were freed on May 27—after four days of captivity—when they were stricken with stomach infection. Four adults at the school and fifty-one on the train were held until June 11, when Dutch commandos struck in two raids. Six terrorists and two hostages died.

On February 27—a little less than three months after the Iranians stormed the U.S. Embassy—guerrillas invaded a diplomatic reception at the embassy of the Dominican Republic in Bogota, Colombia. The guerrillas said they were members of a group called M-19, which took its name from the Colombian presidential elections of April 19, 1970—elections which M-19 claims were rigged.

The guerrillas took fifty-seven hostages, including U.S. Ambassador Diego Asencio. They demanded a ransom of $50 million and publication of their manifesto—neither of which they got.

As the days wore on, the guerrillas released thirty-eight of the hostages. A thirty-ninth captive, the ambassador from Uruguay, escaped. Finally, sixty-one days after the occupation began, the guerrillas left the embassy and flew to Cuba. Four of the remaining sixteen prisoners were freed just before the guerrillas left Colombia. The rest—Asencio among them—were flown to Havana, then released.

Less than one week later, six Iranian Arabs seized the Iranian Embassy in London, taking twenty-six hostages. The gunmen said they wanted freedom for ninety-one Arab-Iranians jailed by Ayatollah Ruhollah Khomeini's government and a flight to safety. Again, the days wore on. Five hostages were released.

The end of the siege came suddenly, six days after it began. The terrorists had abandoned their demand for the release of the prisoners in Iran and British police were hopeful that they could talk the gunmen into giving up.

Shortly before 1:00 P.M. on the sixth day of the crisis, shots were heard inside the embassy. The gunmen announced they had shot one of the hostages and would kill another one every half-hour until their demands were met. More shots were heard. The body of a dead hostage was shoved out the front door of the embassy. Eight commandos, members of the elite Special Air Service regiment, stormed the embassy. The nineteen hostages remaining alive were freed. Only one terrorist survived.

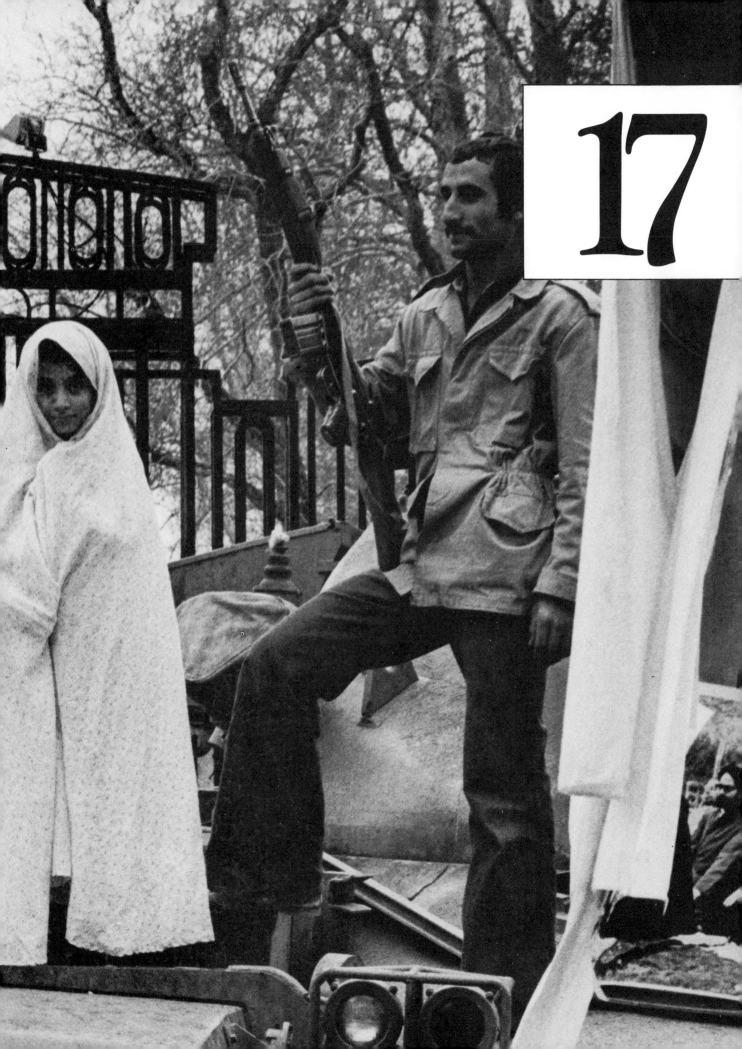

17

"The Empire Strikes Back," a sequel to the movie "Star Wars," premiered. So did a retrospective show of Pablo Picasso at New York's Museum of Modern Art. In Washington, Cyrus Vance had written a letter which he presented to President Carter April 28,

DAY 177

The Secretary of State never did like the rescue mission. Vance had once been second to Robert McNamara in the Pentagon and was not innocent of military matters. Furthermore, he was a lawyer and a diplomatic trouble-shooter. Words sometimes spoke louder than action, he believed.

He questioned the military feasibility of the operation and wanted the Pentagon to demonstrate that it was preferable to the eleven-month-long but ultimately successful negotiations for the release of the Pueblo's crew. Also, the raid was a deliberate deception of America's allies. It possibly endangered 200 Americans still free in Iran, journalists and a few businessmen. The attempt would push Iran closer to the Soviet Union, he feared, and would interrupt United States efforts to obtain bases in Oman and Somalia.

A diplomat, he believed diplomacy was the best chance. He told President Carter as much. On April 16, he argued his case before the National Security Council. The next day, he told Carter if the plan went forward, he would have to resign. On April 21, he wrote by hand a letter to the president to that effect: "Dear Mr. President, I have the greatest respect and admiration for you . . ."

It was no secret he did not have the same esteem for Zbigniew Brzezinski. Carter's brash security adviser was closer, literally, to the president's ear than the State Department and State felt he had usurped the department's traditional role, as it had also felt about Henry Kissinger when he had Brzezinski's job.

"Zbig sometimes sat on Vance's memos to the president for a week before sending them through," said Leslie Gelb, a former senior official at State. This did not make for harmony, although whether it reduced Vance's feelings for Brzezinski to "contempt" was debated.

In any event, when the rescue mission failed, the sixty-three-year-old Vance resigned April 28, feeling honor left him no choice. Carter sent him a formal letter, also in his own hand, in reply. The next day the president named Ed-

mund Muskie, the Democratic senator from Maine, and a member of the Senate Foreign Affairs Committee, to replace Vance.

Then the president announced he was reversing his six-month-old pledge not to campaign for re-election until the hostages were freed. He had come increasingly under attack from Kennedy for his Rose Garden Strategy, which was a natural for political cartoonists. He had already won ninety percent of the delegates necessary for nomination, easily outrunning Kennedy in most the primaries so far. Some said Kennedy should drop out, but he persisted.

The Iranian question was something the contending politicians treated reverently, like motherhood. There was no hunt for heads, as there had been after Nationalist China fell to the Communists. An implied truce seemed to accepted by all concerned as long as the hostages were captive.

Yet when Carter made his first campaign whistlestop, one of his town meetings in Philadelphia which he had cancelled when he withdrew into the Rose Garden in November, there emerged some cutting edges that must have been honed in Iran. For example, he made a rather mean spirited comparison between his old Secretary of State and his new one.

"I see Ed Muskie as being a much stronger and more statesmanlike senior citizen figure who will be a more evocative spokesman for our nation's policy, not nearly so bogged down in the details of administration (of) protocol."

It was a side of Carter the candidate to be heard from not for the last time.

Replacement. Taking up Vance's duties, Edmund S. Muskie, named Secretary of State, is briefed by President Carter one sunny weekend at Camp David.

Casualty. One of the figures who fell by the wayside during the long hostage crisis was Secretary of State Cyrus Vance. He resigned in disagreement over the rescue attempt.

127

18

The world seemed constantly mad. On April 28, some Iranians seized an embassy in London. To the surprise of no one, it was the Iranian Embassy. Not only that, but twenty-one people were taken hostage. This time, however, the captors made good on their death threats on . . .

DAY 184

The militants in Tehran, of course, said the United States was behind the takeover. London, however, seemed an unlikely place for the Great Satan to be at work.

Actually, the six men who seized the embassy were extremists of the Arabic Khuzestan province in southwest Iran, where the oil was. The province had been demanding autonomy. The extremists were demanding the release of ninety-one of their comrades held in Iran.

The embassy under seige was an elegant five-story mansion on Prince's Gate in a posh Kensington neighborhood. The terrorists told police if their demands were not met, they would blow up the building. The British, being the British, cordoned off the area and began talking.

Khomeini, with the sandal now on the other foot, said in Iran that the government would kill one of its prisoners for every one that extremists shot. Ghotbzadeh adapted to this role reversal by declaring, "If Britain cannot do anything, then we will start taking action."

Iranians being Iranians, crowds of them shouted behind the barricades "Khomeini" and "God is Great." British toughs, known as "skinheads" jeered at them.

Chris Cramer, a BBC producer, was one of the hostages who had happened to be in the building. He said, "One of the terrorists kept playing with a hand grenade. He had his finger through the pin the whole time."

Cramer, a Syrian journalist who complained of stomach pains, and three others were released in time. Meanwhile, negotiations continued over the embassy telephone. Patience finally ran low. The extremists said they would start killing a hostage every half-hour if they were not given a bus ride to the airport.

One of the hostages, twenty-five-year-old Abbas Labasani, had volunteered to be the first to die. He was taken downstairs.

"After the first shot, I heard a cry, something like a loud grunt of 'Ha,'" said Muhammad Hashir Faruqi of Pakistan, a British journalist who was a hostage. "I think the one who killed Labasani was the gunman I called 'the ugly one.' He appeared to be angry all the time."

Labasani's body was thrown out the front door. The British ran out of patience.

There was in the British military, a unit called the Special Air Service regiment. It had been organized in 1941 for raids behind German lines. Now its specialty was anti-terrorist activities and it had on-the-job training in Northern Ireland. About a dozen SAS commandos had been studying diagrams of the embassy for days. Now they were sent into action.

British negotiators said they would agree to the extremists' terms. Their leader, who called himself Salim Towfigh, began making arrangements on the phone for a bus. Hostage Trevor Lock, a constable who had been on duty at the embassy, and another hostage Englishman, BBC soundman Simeon Harris, assured their captors the police would not try to rush the building. Then there was the sound of breaking glass.

The commandos came shinnying down on ropes and burst through the windows. One of the Arabs began spraying a room filled with hostages with machine-gun fire. He missed everybody. Two other terrorists came in shooting—killing one embassy employee and wounding Dr. Gholam Ali Afrouz, the Chargé d'affaires.

The commandos threw in stun grenades. "That was it," said Harris. "I got myself out the back. To my right there was a man dressed like a frogman, complete black mask, black uniform, black boots. He said, 'Get down, get down, get down!' I lay down flat. He kicked the window in and threw two crackers in. He was followed by two men, and I was completely overjoyed. I felt no fear then."

"It's the kind of thing you see only in films."

The commandos rounded up the hostages. The extremists had been trying to conceal themselves among them. The Iranians pointed two of them out. "The SAS shot them dead," said Faruqi. Another terrorist had been about to shoot a commando who was tangled in his rope. Constable Lock tackled him first. The commando shot him. When it was over, live on British TV, only one terrorist survived.

Prime Minister Margaret Thatcher said the successful attack "made us all proud to be British." Then she stopped by to have a beer with the commandos.

Dr. Afrouz was asked later if he saw any similarities between his being held hostage in London and the Americans in Tehran. "No parallel at all," he said. The Americans "have been our guests."

Lunchtime. One of the Iranian dissidents stepped warily out of the London Embassy to fetch a parcel of food left on the doorstep by police. Lamb chops and Persian delicacies from a nearby restaurant.

QUOTES

The words of those most deeply involved—hostages, revolutionaries, diplomats and politicians—in many ways told the story of the Iran hostage crisis. They are words of anger and frustration, sadness and helplessness. But often, too, the words spoke of perseverance and courage. Here is the story of the crisis in its own words:

"We will continue to stay here and won't release any of the hostages until the United States returns the ousted Shah, which is what the Iranian people want." —A young Iranian revolutionary after he and his comrades seize the U.S. Embassy, Tehran.

"There is no way this government can or will negotiate under the gun of its own people being held hostage." —U.S. State Department spokesman Hodding Carter.

"He said the United States will turn the screws a little tighter every few days." —An anonymous U.S. Congressman, speaking of President Carter after the United States imposed sanctions on Iran.

"This is a war between Moslems and pagans." —Ayatollah Ruhollah Khomeini.

"The American people are seething with anger." —U.S. Ambassador Donald F. McHenry to the U.N. Security Council.

"We're not ready to hold out here forever." —Hostage William Gallegos, a Marine, in a televised statement.

"They are being treated in a manner pleasing to God." —Ayatollah Ruhollah Khomeini.

"There were tears in their eyes." —The Rev. William Sloane Coffin, after conducting Christmas services for the hostages.

"If ever we needed a doctor, we need one now . . . We pray the Lord will be with us and give us strength so we may go home soon before we all go crazy." —Hostage Johnny McKeel Jr., in a letter after Christmas 1979.

"I am glad to be back, especially alive." —U.N. Secretary-General Kurt Waldheim, returning to New York after an unsuccessful mediation trip to Tehran.

"Although we could only hold off the attack on the embassy for three hours, we have still maintained the high standards of America. We are all proud to be Americans." —Hostage Joseph Subic Jr., an Army staff sergeant, in a letter.

"From the moment when the people give me their confidence, there will be no major difficulties because this affair of the hostages is a minor affair." —Abolhassan Bani-Sadr, on his election as Iranian president.

"Thank You, Canada. Merci Beaucoup." —Billboards on the U.S.-Canadian border after Canadian diplomats spirited six Americans out of Tehran.

"The longer I am held, the more I've come to despise my captors and what harm they've done myself and all my family by taking my freedom without me ever having done an Iranian any harm." —Hostage Donald Hohman, an Army medic, in a letter.

"Some of the hostages are mentally distressed." —Unidentified Iranian doctor who visited the hostages.

"Late yesterday I canceled a carefully planned operation which was under way in Iran. . . ." —President Carter telling the nation of the tragic failure of a U.S. commando rescue mission in Iran.

"We have decided to keep the hostages in custody in various cities through the country . . . to deprive the criminal Carter of his pretext for such aggression." —The embassy militants, announcing the scattering of the hostages outside Tehran.

"The court unanimously decides that the government of the Islamic Republic of Iran . . . must immediately terminate the unlawful detention of the United States chargé d'affaires and other diplomatic and consular staff and other United States nationals now held hostage in Iran." —The World Court.

"I believe in Providence. All depends on that." —The exiled Shah Mohammad Reza Pahlavi, asked about his future.

"Life as a hostage sort of became life itself." —Hostage Richard Queen after his release.

"The hostage taking is a revolutionary action that has frightened America completely. We should take revolutionary advantage of the act."

"It (Iran's war with Iraq) may knock some sense into them." —Freed hostage Richard Queen.

"In the name of God, the compassionate, the merciful: the special commission investigating the issue of the American spies submits the following proposals to the Islamic consultative assembly, according to the guidelines of the Imam." —The Iranian Parliament, finally voting on the hostage issue.

"I sincerely wish . . . that this Christmas time can be a time of change and new hope and perhaps, with a little effort on everybody's part, it will lead to peace on Earth and good will among all men." —Hostage David Roeder in a filmed Christmas 1980 message.

"That would be pretty foolish." —Ronald Reagan, commenting on an Iranian suggestion that Iran might wait for his inauguration before trying to negotiate an end to the crisis.

"It appears that the date for the release of the hostages is approaching." —Iranian official Ahmed Azizi.

"The hostages are like a fruit from which all the juice has been squeezed." —Iranian negotiator Behzad Nabavi, to the Iranian Parliament.

"My God, it's over. It's finished and they're coming home." —Dorothea Morefield, wife of hostage Richard Morefield.

Another name to remember.
Iranian Premier Mohammad Ali Rajai.

MOHAMMAD ALI RAJAI

Mohammad Ali Rajai in some ways epitomizes the Iranian revolution—fervently Islamic, staunchly nationalist and untainted by Western "corruption."

Rajai, age forty-seven, was named prime minister in August 1980 by a reluctant President Abolhassan Bani-Sadr only because the Islamic Republican Party forced the choice on him. The president, in fact, told his followers he believed the new prime minister was not up to the job and was too headstrong and contentious.

The president and prime minister's first clash came quickly—over Rajai's nominees for Cabinet positions, men Bani-Sadr considered too young and inexperienced in political affairs.

Rajai himself—rough-shaven, mustachioed and plainly dressed—had less than a year's government experience, as acting education minister. By profession he is a math teacher.

He was born in the northern Iranian city of Qazvin and was educated there and in Tehran, where he obtained a bachelor of science degree in mathematics.

While teaching school in Qazvin and Tehran, he became politically active in the Islam-inspired movement against the regime of Shah Mohammad Reza Pahlavi. The dissidents protested Pahlavi's attempts to Westernize Iran's traditionally Moslem life, to dilute the power of the clergy and to ally Iran with the United States militarily and economically.

Rajai was arrested twice for his political activities, serving a prison term of two months in the 1960s and a four-year term in the 1970s, during which he reportedly was tortured by Pahlavi's SAVAK secret police. He was not released until late 1978, just before Ayatollah Ruhollah Khomeini's revolution triumphed after months of bloodshed.

Upon his selection as prime minister, Rajai reaffirmed his militant fervor, saying that the Iranian government must be kept in the hands of "the revolutionaries who stood before bullets."

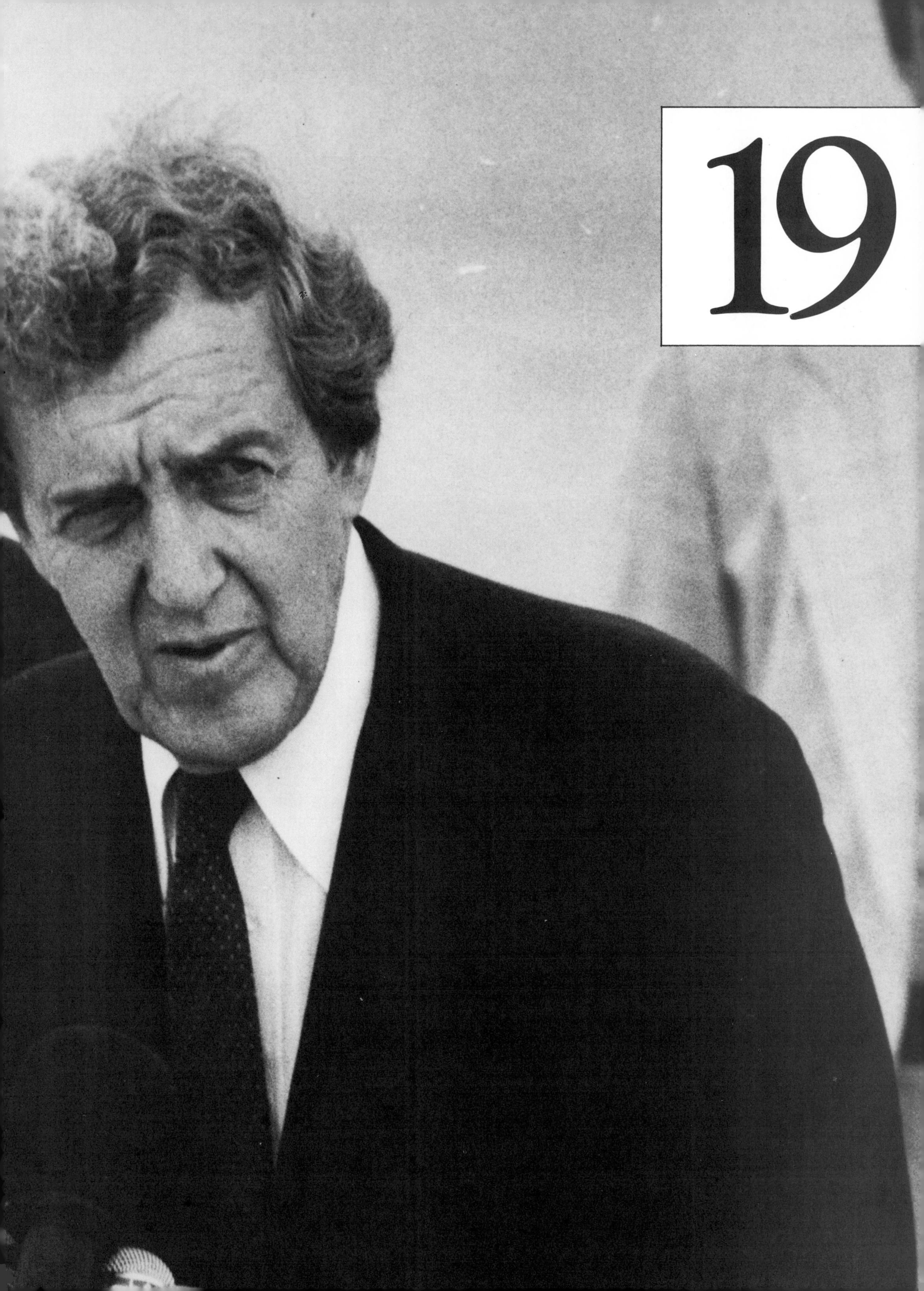

19

Ronald Reagan was about to be annointed in Detroit, the sputtering Motor City. The Russians were about to open the Olympics in Moscow despite a U.S. boycott protesting the invasion of Afghanistan. Gerry Ford was almost, but not about to be a vice presidential candidate. The fifty-three hostages were about to become fifty-two on . . .

DAY 250

During the Easter visit, twenty-eight-year-old Richard Queen, the consular officer, had told the American clergymen his fingers had been turning numb. As weeks passed, he became nauseous and dizzy. A new beard did not conceal a loss of weight. Queen, who had organized a library for the hostages, was finally taken to a hospital.

On July 10, Khomeini announced that Queen would be coming out. Accompanied by the Swiss ambassador, who handled U.S. affairs in Tehran, he was flown to Zurich, then to an Air Force hospital in Wiesbaden, Germany, where his condition was ultimately described as multiple sclerosis.

There he reunited with his parents, Harold Queen, a retired executive of RCA, and his wife, Jeanne. They greeted their son was some raspberries, a bunch of roses and a rosary.

"Richard is not as we have known him a year ago," said his father. "His mind is very good, but he's very weak, very weak." But others who talked with him were surprised at "how normal he sounded and solid."

Queen was told not to talk too freely, but he said some of the hostages had become deeply depressed. Fit once again to travel, Richard Queen flew home to be greeted in Washington by Muskie, his new boss.

"I really can't express with words what it's like to be in America again," he said. "I just wish there were fifty-two more with me."

Later, Queen discussed his capture while relaxing at his family's new home in Maine, a house he had never seen.

In the early days the militants had staged mock executions of some of the hostages, pulling the triggers on guns that turned out to be unloaded. Other Iranians were helpful, fetching books or clothing. Some harassed them by not responding to their requests to go the bathroom. Some were "really fine people," a few "real SOBs."

Queen confided that he thought at times he wasn't going to be able to go on. But a fellow American marvelled at Queen's imperturbability. "You're a perfect hostage," he said.

Queen lived in a basement room he called "Mushroom Inn." He would be taken for exercise occasionally, his view shielded by a blanket over his head. Once he realized he was being led in a different direction. When the blanket was removed, he was standing against a wall. "I just thought, 'Oh, oh, this is the end.' "

He read copiously of Shakespeare and histories of the Civil War. "I cursed myself for speaking Farsi. Whenever they talked, I closed my ears." But once, in December, he heard militants talking on the phone. They seemed to be making plane reservations. The hostages thought they were going home and began lining up for showers. "Getting up the next day and realizing, no, we were not going home, that was the worst moment."

Afterwards he overheard some of the students cursing the foreign ministry. But the Iranians were a determined group. "One of them told me with a straight face that in fifty years the United States would be an Islamic republic."

• • •

Since everyone else seemed to have a spokesman, the families of the hostages got one too: themselves. Organized as the Family Liaison Action Group Inc., (FLAG) they had been given an office at the State Department and later moved to a suite donated by a law firm.

Some day there would no longer be a need for a FLAG, they hoped. Then any money left would go to charity. On the other hand, they might keep going as a permanent organization helping future hostage families.

"Unfortunately," said Louisa Kennedy, "we're in the age of terrorists."

• • •

For forty-eight hours all traffic out of Iran was shut down. It was something called "Red Alert," not a test, but the real thing—an attempt to overthrow Khomeini's Revolutionary Council and reinstall Shahpur Bakhtiar, the Shah's last prime minister.

Phantom jets were to have bombed Tehran's airports as well as Khomeini's house in Qum. Putschists were also to seize the national television and radio headquarters. Bani-Sadr and Ghotzbzadeh were to be arrested along with other leaders and executed. In all, about 1,000 Iranians, civilian and military, were reportedly involved. One of the conspirators defected, however, and the plot was revealed. Mass arrests followed.

The following week, three gunmen posing as reporters tried to kill Bakhtiar in his Paris apartment. They failed, but a police guard and a neighbor were killed in the shooting.

Did Rip Van Winkle in the compound know? Were doves still coming to the window ledges?

One for the road. Richard Queen is greeted by Secretary of State Muskie after the Iranians released him from the hostage pool for health reasons.

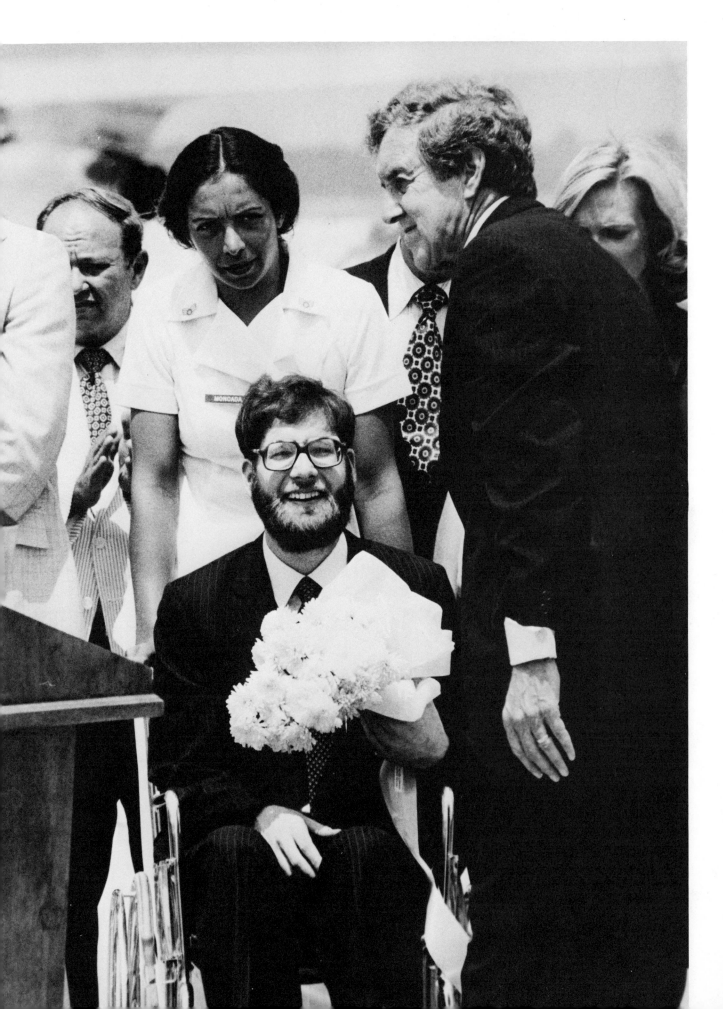

20

Billy Carter's shenanigans with the Libyans were making more headlines than his brother. Peter Sellers died. The American Southwest sizzled in record heat. Romanian gymnast Nadia Comaneci, the teen-aged star at Montreal, fell at the Moscow Olympics. The Shah was gravely ill in Cairo on . . .

DAY 267

At 4 A.M. he was fully conscious. Six hours later he was dead. The thirty-eight year reign of Shah Mohammed Reza Pahlavi had come to an end in a hospital in Cairo. For the last eighteen months of his life the Light of the Aryans had been a man without a country.

Iran Radio gloated: "The bloodsucker of the century has died at last." The newspaper *Etela'at* attributed his death to the CIA. Once the Shah was offstage, it was felt, the United States could get its hostages home.

Washington said blandly when the sixty-year-old Shah died July 27: "His death marks the end of an era in Iran which all hope will be followed by peace and stability." Another deposed leader, Richard Nixon, sent "deepest sympathy" to the family and said he would go to Cairo for the funeral.

A Khomeini spokesman in Tehran said, "Since the Shah's death was predictable, it won't change anything concerning Iranian-American relations and the hostages."

The Shah had been in Egypt since March, a guest of President Sadat. Egypt had been the only country willing to give him refuge in his final days. Since June 27 the Shah had been in Maadi Military Hospital where he had been operated on at least three times for his cancer. He had become frail, jaundiced and feverish. His pancreas had begun hemorrhaging from an abscess which, rather than workings of the CIA, led to his death.

It was a bitter end for a man who had tried to cast his nation into a mold of his own devising. He had castigated the West self-righteously for wastefulness, particularly of his own country's oil. Yet he sold that oil for the highest price he could extract to bedeck his poor country with more costly technology, particularly armaments, than it could afford. He, as the Ayatollah, said he had been "chosen by God" to lead his people. And he brutalized them when they would not follow.

For seven years, Fereydoun Hoveida had been the Shah's ambassador to the United Nations. He wrote a book called *The Fall of the Shah*.

"He was essentially a weak man who played the role of a dictator," Hoveida said. "Tragically, the Shah's reforms were eclipsed within a few years by his increasing authoritarianism. In his consuming passion for what he conceived of as his divine mission, he came to believe in his own infallibility."

"He ruled as a lion and a fox," said James Bill, a specialist on Iran at the University of Texas.

Said Nixon: "Now that his personal ordeal is over, the government of Iran has no excuse whatsoever for continuing to hold innocent American hostages."

Not so. There was still the matter of the Shah's money.

•　　　•　　　•

In Tehran, there was increasing confusion as to who would succeed to the Shah's mantle. A Majlis had been chosen, and Khomeini had said the fate of the hostages would be left in its hands. He seemed increasingly distant from President Bani-Sadr. "None of our ministries are proper ones," he complained and said the Majlis must appoint a new government that would be "one-hundred percent Islamic."

A number of leaders of the July 7 failed coup by Bakhtiar supporters had been put to death. There were mutterings in the streets now, no longer shouting crowds. Women who refused to cover themselves in the street complained they were "treated like prostitutes." Numbers of them were removed from their jobs. Inflation and shortages worsened. A 7th century theocracy imposed on a 20th century technocracy that had been trying to impose itself on a 19th century feudal society did not make for good arithmetic.

•　　　•　　　•

Almost as forgotten as the hostages in the internal Iranian political struggle were the people who held them, the militants. They had become almost as much prisoners as their captives. They were confined to the embassy lest they be contaminated by those outside the walls. To keep their faith burning, they held daily prayer sessions and pep talks. One had complained to Richard Queen that he was missing his classes. "Oh, that's too bad," Queen said sarcastically.

Some of the guards had begun playing ping-pong and Scrabble with their captives. But they let little news of the outside world filter in. One guard the Americans called Hamid the Liar denied that ninety bags of mail had not been delivered.

"He was a child," Richard Queen recalled. "Hamid said it was all the CIA's fault." Hamid the Liar eventually went elsewhere.

◄ "The Shah Is Dead." The guards at the hostage embassy hold a newspaper with the news. Hope for the hostage release rose again.

Funeral in Egypt. Former President Richard M. Nixon escorts Empress Farah in the funeral procession in Cairo where the Shah died and was buried. ▼

Meanwhile, Sgt. Michael Moeller, one of the Marines, had a problem. The Iranian Justice Ministry said in the spring it was going to try him for having sexual relations with an unmarried twenty-three-year-old Iranian woman, a crime punishable by up to ten years in prison. The government said Moeller had seduced her before the takeover. They had met when she came to the embassy for English lessons. The woman, identified only as Amaz A., had been hanged by her brother when he learned she was pregnant. Moeller denied the charges.

*   *   *

The day the Shah died, one-hundred-and-ninety-three Iranians were arrested near the White House in a violent demonstration. Ten days later they were released.

21

Good old summer time. So what if wells in the East were running dry? If unemployment was 8.2 million? If Jimmy Carter's popularity rating was an all-time low? If inflation was at an all-time high? So what? George Brett was slugging .400, wasn't he? It was good old summer time. August. It was also...

MONTH 10

J.R. Ewing was shot March 21, 1980, Day 139. Who shot him was meant to be revealed when TV's evening "Dallas" premiered for the new season September 19. That would be Day 321.

That was a gap of 182 days, almost half a year. A half of a year that Americans lived while Rip Van Winkle slept. Did Rip know that:

Teddy Kennedy had lost?

That Ronald Reagan had won and chosen the man he beat, George Bush, as his running mate?

That while the high heat of summer baked Tehran, the first trial of something called Abscam had begun? Abscam?

That striking workers in Gdansk, Poland, were toppling a government that had denied workers in the workers' paradise the right to unionize?

That Billy Carter told a Congressional committee that he hoped his testimony would show he wasn't "a buffoon, a boob, or a wacko"?

Did they know that their country had been counted, as the Constitution requires, and that there were 226,504,825 Americans present and accounted for?

Did anyone count them, the 52 Rip Van Winkles?

They, for their part, had not forgotten. Don Hohman wrote his Dad:

"Don't worry about me because I'm tough and stubborn enough to take anything these pinheads can dish out. I'm a Hohman."

Joseph Hall to his sister:

"I realize this will go on for a while, but you must know I am handling the situation with as much Hall dignity as I can muster. Call it the ability to cope, acceptance of the inevitable or whatever you like. I WILL come through this ordeal O.K."

Keough had written his daughters after the first three months: "I also hope you are saving clippings for me so that I'll be able to understand why President Carter has left us here. I find it so hard to believe."

Did a dove at the window ever bring word from Desert One?

The Pentagon issued its report of the rescue attempt on August 23. The effort could have benefited by having two additional helicopters. Weather forecasters might have briefed the pilots on the potential for a sandstorm. They didn't, so as to keep security at a maximum. An Iranian forecast would have tipped the operation's destination. The sky had been clear at Desert One. The pilot who turned back said he would have kept going had he know that. The report faulted the raid for confusion on the ground, due in part to lack of a full dress rehearsal.

"We encountered not a shred of evidence of culpable neglect or incompetence," concluded the head of the investigation, former Chief of Naval Operations James L. Holloway III.

The file was closed on Desert One on Day 294.

Johnny McKeel, Marine, wrote:

"If we ever needed a doctor, we need one now. Most of us have lost between fifteen and twenty-five pounds. Trying to sleep is really hard."

Michael Lopez, Marine from Arizona:

"Mom, I have this almost uncontrollable craving for a beef tamale."

Bob Ode, the exercise biker:

"We have no idea what is being done..."

Doubt, frustration, perseverance. Fifty-two not home when the census taker dropped by. Time lost to be filled with clippings. But you had to have been there, really, to have lived it.

The kickoff of the new season of "Dallas" wasn't until November 21. It had been held up by a strike of the Screen Actors Guild. That was on Day 384 and counting.

Kristin Shepard shot J.R.

Campaign '80. It went on as usual, but there were 52 Americans who didn't get to vote.

22

The Kansas City Royals led their division. There was no second. The Yankees were up and down but always first. The National League was a tossup in both divisions. And Secretary Muskie wrote a letter.

DAY 302

The letter was delivered to Iran's new prime minister, Ali Rajai, August 31.

Rajai was the latest in what seemed to have been a game of musical chairs. But with his appointment by Bani-Sadr on August 9, Day 280, the government in Tehran took on an appearance of lasting longer than the next sandstorm. The Majlis, albeit dominated by Moslem clerics, was in business. And Bani-Sadr had long been on record for wanting to put the hostage crisis behind him and to try and cure the chaos of his nation.

Inflation was running at seventy or eighty percent. Executions in the wake of the July coup attempt symbolized the fragility of the internal stability of the country—in London, Amnesty International estimated from 1,000 to 1,500 people had been put to death since Khomeini took over. Along the Iraqi border there were persistent incidents. And in the face of all this, Iran stood isolated in the world. The Western boycott of Iranian oil "hasn't brought anyone to his knees," said a U.S. official, but it pinched.

Muskie had some grounds to think it was time for a new diplomatic initiative. The stubborn Mainer, once a presidential candidate himself, was no stranger to cloakroom horse trading. Now he was putting his expertise to use— quietly—on an international level.

He perceived that a government was gradually emerging in Iran that had enough continuity to be approached. He saw the release of Richard Queen as a favorable omen. Tehran was not totally heartless to humanitarian need. The month–long fast of Ramadan was concluding, a time for renewal.

The contents of Muskie's letter were not disclosed. It was learned that he had asked for release of the hostages but had not "apologized" for U.S. intervention in Iran as the Majlis had demanded. There was one ray of hope, however. Rajai indicated he would answer Muskie's letter.

A dialogue, to whatever extent, had begun.

* * *

One familiar face was about to drop from view. Rajai said he was going to replace Ghotbzadeh as foreign minister. But before departing the scene, Ghotbzadeh had some refreshingly candid things to say from the United States' point of view.

Trials of the hostages, he said, "would be against the national interests" of Iran. "Our demand, the extradition of the Shah, has become irrelevant. But obviously we cannot let the hostages go without first having the United States give us back what it has taken from us. The $8.5 billion seized by the United States is ours. Its return to Iran needs no negotiation. Some U.S. companies have obtained court orders for freezing Iranian assets against debts which they claim we own them. (There were some 230 such suits involving billions of dollars. The Carter Administration was trying to postpone action on them until release of the hostages.) Such claims should be considered. If we really owe them money, we will pay it. We don't want anything more than we are rightfully entitled to. (But) the wealth the Shah plundered from Iran is ours without any shadow of doubt. These details must be negotiated. What matters in the final analysis is a clear, honest discussion of these problems."

They don't waste words in Maine. Neither had Ghotbzadeh.

* * *

The Majlis, controlled by the fundamentalist Islamic Republican Party, was another matter. Fundamentalist it might be, but this did not put it above political arm wrestling.

Bani-Sadr was not happy with the dismissal of Ghotbzadeh. "I approve of several members of the (Rajai's) Cabinet but not of others." Ghotbzadeh criticized the choice of Rajai. "He is a good Moslem and devout revolutionary, but he is incapable of running the country." As for the Majlis, he said, "the problem is that it has gone so far out on a limb in its quest for radical gestures that it will have difficulty in regaining its poise."

The parliament itself had not yet decided when to take up the matter of the hostages. It had received a letter from 187 U.S. Congressmen asking for their release. In response, the Foreign Affairs Commission of the Majlis drafted a letter saying: "Gentlemen, you can take positive steps in resolving the hostage crisis. You can place on your urgent agenda the assessment of the damages sustained by Iran because of U.S. policies and Iran's legitimate demands, especially the return of the assets of the Shah and his relatives. It is in this way that the path to the settlement of the crisis will be opened."

The reply, however, was ordered shelved by Majlis Speaker Akbar Hashemi Rafsanjani, a fundamentalist's fun-

The voices keep changing. Replacing Bani-Sadr as foreign minister is Sadegh Ghotbzadeh who takes a firmer stand on the hostages.

damentalist. He said there should be a wider representation of parliamentary opinion.

If Tehran felt hemmed in, it had good reason. Iraq was hostile to the west of Iran. Russia had overrun Afghanistan to the east. Her army was an uncertain trumpet, witness the coup attempt. The Shah's shiny American jets were not much use without spare parts and trained technicians to maintain them. Iran was rather naked to her enemies.

"The Soviets are going to inordinate lengths to make sure Iran sinks deeper and deeper into international isolation," said Ghotbzadeh. "Their policy is clear: to bludgeon Iran to its knees and then impose on it whatever conditions they want."

"The main problem is the Tudeh (Communist) Party, which, at the bidding of Moscow, drives the young generation to political sabotage."

He did not say if he had the militants at the embassy in mind, but he blamed Iran's isolation in part on "the blind radicalism of our youths. They are revolutionary idealists out to put everything right overnight."

•　　　•　　　•

Everyone was talking, and that was hopeful. But the Ayatollah was the ultimate piper who called the tunes. And he had not spoken from on high regarding the hostages since February.

He finally broke his silence in a message broadcast by Tehran radio on September 12. That was Day 314. For the first time Khomeini was laying down terms. They were:

1. Return the property of the Shah.
2. Cancel all U.S. claims against Iran.
3. Stay out of Iranian affairs.
4. Unfreeze the assets.

Notably, Khomeini made no mention of spy trials nor a U.S. apology for "crimes" in Iran.

Condition number three was easy. Muskie had said in his August letter that the United States would "respect" Iranian independence. The Shah's wealth was another matter. Iran's Central Bank said it amounted to $32 billion. American officials estimated it was more like $60 million to $100 million, location undetermined but most probably not all in the United States. Most probably not much in the United States. In any case, not even the President of the United States can write checks on someone else's bank account. The Iranians, newcomers to the ways of republics, might possibly have a hard time grasping that.

The Ayatollah did not forget to include fire and brimstone. The United States, he said, "sucks the blood of unprotected people." But amidst all the customary hot sauce, there was some meat. And what it came down to in essence was what had been present all along: a matter of money.

In San Diego, Richard Morefield's wife reminded everybody that the Iranians were "a nation of rug merchants." If so, they were beginning to show their true nature. They were beginning to haggle.

•　　　•　　　•

Jimmy Carter, a patient fisherman, did not snap at the bait. Nor did he spurn it. "We've learned to be very cautious about statements from Iran," he said.

He did not have to go further than the Majlis to get a second opinion on Khomeini's proposals.

"We do not compromise or make deals," Rajai declared. The United States must first come to the bargaining table purged by making the six Moslem steps of repentance, including fasting "so that your body will be cleansed of all that you have eaten that is forbidden by religion. But, if we were sure you had repented, we would talk." The remark was not a needle's eye that a camel could readily squeeze through, but it had the key words: we would talk.

In order to talk with someone you have severed talking relations with, you must have a go-between. One possibility was Algeria, which had been representing Iran in Washington. Or possibly the Swiss who did the same for the United States in Tehran.

Another interested party was Ronald Reagan, who might some day inherit Carter's hotseat. He took a stance on Khomeini's terms that was not to change during the increasingly bare-knuckled presidential campaign. He would support negotiations on Iran's conditions except for the Shah's money, which he said was a matter for the courts. Should Carter reach an agreement before inauguration day January 20, Day 444, and he was the inauguree, he would "observe the terms," he added.

Reagan's camp had been apprehensive that the long arm of the Ayatollah might reach into the presidential race. Believing Carter to be the lesser of two Satans, Khomeini might create "an October surprise" by freeing the hostages in time for Carter to capitalize on a surge of popular approval.

The White House said it would not "stay up all night" devising a reply to Khomeini, but it was working with a little more optimism during the day.

In Balch Springs, Texas, hostage Johnny McKeel's father was skeptical. He said the Ayatollah's offer was "a whole lot of bull."

Richard Queen, if anybody in America, knew the weight of the Ayatollah's words in Iran. Take them seriously? "It can't hurt," he said.

OTHER HOSTAGE INCIDENTS

The West Germans formed a special unit to deal with terrorists after the 1972 Olympics in Munich, when eight Palestinians sneaked into the sleeping quarters of the Israeli team. Two athletes were killed and nine were taken hostage. The Palestinians demanded freedom for their comrades in Israeli jails and a flight to the Middle East.

German officials took the gunmen and their captives, via helicopter, to a military airport. Sharpshooters waited to pick off the Palestinians, but hit only two of them. One of the six remaining terrorists tossed a grenade into a helicopter where the Israelis sat, bound and blindfolded. All nine hostages were killed before the terrorists were captured.

The commando unit that was formed as a result of the Munich disaster went into action at Mogadishu, Somalia, in October 1977.

Four Arab terrorists had hijacked a Lufthansa Airlines plane en route from Mallorca to Frankfurt with more than eighty people aboard. The attack was staged in conjunction with the earlier kidnapping of a West German industrialist. The hijackers and the kidnappers wanted freedom for a dozen terrorists in West German jails.

The plane flew to Rome, Nicosia, Baharain, Abu Dhabi, Aden and finally, four days after it was hijacked, to Mogadishu. Along the way, the chief pilot had been killed.

Less than twenty-four hours after the plane reached Mogadishu, the German commandos went into operation. They stormed the plane, killed three of the hijackers and freed the eighty-six hostages. The industrialist was found dead the next day in France.

An Israeli commando team rescued hostages in Africa more than a year earlier—at Entebbe, Uganda. On June 27, 1976, four terrorists—two Palestinians and two West Germans—commandeered an Air France flight from Tel Aviv to Paris when it stopped at Athens to refuel. The plane was refueled in Libya, then flown to Entebbe where the terrorists—demanding the release of fifty-three prisoners from jails in five countries—brought in reinforcements.

The hijackers freed 148 hostages, but continued to hold ninety four Jewish passengers and twelve Air France crew members. On July 3, the Israeli commandos burst into the terminal building where the captives were held. Less than an hour later, the hostages were on their way home. One commando, seven terrorists and twenty Ugandan soldiers were killed.

A rescue effort by Egyptian commandos was less successful. The commandos were trying to free hostages taken during an Afro-Asian conference in Nicosia, Cyprus, in February 1978.

The terrorists had traded some of their hostages in exchange for safe conduct to Lancara Airport and took off in a Cyprus Airways plane with a volunteer crew of four and eleven hostages. The terrorists were turned away from several countries in their quest for a safe haven. The plane returned to Lancara. Egyptian commandos stormed the plane, but Cypriot troops opened fire on them, killing more than a dozen. Meanwhile, the terrorists had surrendered to the plane's crew and had freed the hostages.

Most of the hostages who have been taken were seized overseas, but terrorists also have struck in the United States. Early in 1977, a dozen Hanafi Moslem terrorists involved in a feud with a rival Black Muslim group took 134 hostages at three separate sites in Washington, D.C. Those hostages were held for thirty-eight hours before the gunmen surrendered. One person was killed and four were wounded during the siege.

23

Assassins blew up former Nicaraguan dictator Anastasio Somoza in exile in Paraguay. John Lennon told an interviewer reviving the Beatles would be retrogression, "like going back to school." Iraq claimed it had shot down two Iranian jets in border skirmishes on . . .

DAY 320

Finally, after all those months, the Majlis began debating about the hostages.

One member, Ali Agha Mohammadi, gave a blistering harangue. "We will try the spy hostages according to the Moslem code that says the punishment for a spy is death! The first one to be tries in the one who dropped the bombs on Vietnam." That was Lt.Col. Roeder.

But the Majlis instead voted to turn the issue over to a special commission.

The only trouble was the commission hadn't been **named yet.**

Majlis Speaker Rafsanjani holds a press conference on January 12, Day 436 and says that "all roads" are open to a settlement.

153

24

Ronald Reagan and John Anderson held a debate in Baltimore. Jimmy Carter decided not to come. The government warned women that tampons could be fatal to their health. A young blonde executive quit the Bendix Corp. in the wake of rumors about how to succeed in business. The Persian Gulf was producing forty percent of the free world's oil until . . .

DAY 324

September 22 was perhaps the day the hostages started to come home.

On that day, Ayatollah Khomeini found a new Satan in his neighbor, President Saddam Hussein of Iraq. The two Moslem nations went to war, and the hostages suddenly became a much larger bargaining chip in isolated, American-armed Iran.

The border incidents that culminated in the Iraqi attack had been recent but the causes were of ancient origin, dating back to when Hussein, Mohammed's grandson, was slain on his way to Baghdad. The Shiites of Iran had never forgotten the Iraqi treachery, even though a majority of that nation's people were of the same branch of Islam. A more recent provocation was the 1975 agreement more or less forced on Iraq by the Shah, giving Iran partial control of the Shatt al Arab, the strategic waterway from the confluence of the Tigris and Euphrates rivers into the Persian Gulf. It was Iraq's only link to the sea. Through it moved much of the 2.2 million barrels produced daily by Iraq, the world's second largest exporter.

Hussein had surrendered part of the waterway in exchange for the Shah's agreement to stop supporting a rebellion among the Kurds in Iraq.

On September 17, 1980, Hussein abrogated the treaty. Five days later his forces struck. The fighting shut off most oil shipments from both nations, as each attacked the other's wells and refineries. Now the entire free world was directly involved in the events in Tehran.

One of the initial targets of the Iraqi army was the city of Adaban on the Shatt al Arab. It was the site of one of the largest refineries in the world, its daily capacity of 587,000 barrels providing the bulk of Iran's oil needs. Iraqi units also made for the Iranian seaport of Khorramshahr, upstream from Abadan.

On paper, Iran held the stronger hand. Its army consisted of 415,000 men, 1,700 tanks and 447 planes. Iraq's

army was put at 222,000, tanks at 1,800 with 339 planes, mostly Russian. But Iran's army had been depleted by the revolution and many of its generals shot. Of seventy-seven topflight American F-14s, only seven or eight were deemed flyable, according to Western estimates. What was imponderable, however, was whether or not the fanaticism Khomeini's mobs brought to the streets could be translated to the battlefield.

As air raid sirens whined through Tehran one night, militants ran to rooftops to fire into the air, shake their fists and cry "Allahu akbar!" (God is great). It turned out to be only a drill. A real raid destroyed a Phantom at Tehran's Mehrabad Airport. Iranian F-4s and F-5Es retaliated by attacking Baghdad. Three Americans were killed in a strafing raid on a petrochemical plant being built at Basra on the Iraq side of Shatt al Arab.

"There is a spirit of unity coming back, just like during the revolution," said an Iranian mother in Tehran. Militiamen headed for the front. Bani-Sadr, as commander in chief, paid them a visit. Even the Shah's eldest son, a student in Cairo and a qualified fighter pilot, volunteered to defend the homeland.

Khomeini stopped further trials of military men and assured his soldiers they would all go to heaven if they died in battle. He told Iraqi Shiites to "paralyze the economy. Stop paying taxes. This is war between Islam and blasphemy. If you can kill Saddam before we can execute him, stab him in the back."

The Iraqis said their goals were limited. They sought sovereignty of Shatt al Arab, about 320 square miles of Iranian territory around the town of Musian and three small islands in the Strait of Hormuz, the key to the Persian Gulf, which the Shah had seized in 1971 from the United Arab Emigrates.

But the Iranians were showing surprising resistance as the blood of the world's lifeline—oil—went up in smoke.

* * *

Of course, the United States was behind the Iraq attack. Bani-Sadr said as much, anyway. He did not think the war would affect the hostages for the time being. "But if the international situation gets worse, it could get worse for the hostages. We have heard the Americans are sending military aid to the Iraqis. If so, the hostage situation will certainly worsen."

Carter said the United States would remain strictly neutral. "We have not been and we will not become involved in the conflict between Iran and Iraq," he said. But he said his nation, which had twenty-eight warships in the

Another flag. An Iraqi trooper holds his own nation's emblem atop an Iranian building.

area as part of the expanding American deployment in the Indian Ocean, would do "whatever is required" to keep the Strait of Hormuz open.

Bani-Sadr said he would seek no help from United States nor the Soviet Union. But to fight a war costs money. Iran had money in the bank. But the bank was in the United States. It didn't require a rug merchant to figure one way to get the money out.

25

The war went on. If their claims were to be believed, Iraq and Iran had shot down all each other's planes three times over. Men were dying, oil facilities were in ruins, gasless Tehranis were walking while their prime minister came to the United States on...

DAY 349

Mohammed Ali Rajai could be said to be an enemy to a razor blade or a necktie as well as to Iraq and the United States.

But, unshaven and unbibbed, the Iranian number three man stood before the United Nations in New York on October 17 and gave a well-tailored rendition of how American "imperialism" was supporting Iraq's invasion of his country. For sixty-five minutes he pled his case, only once referring to the hostages.

"How is it that the United States sees in this attack an opportunity for its hostages to be freed?" he said.

Rajai had refused to see Carter—the president had been willing—to get his own answers, but the next day he provided some of his own at a news conference. He said the Majlis would decide on the hostages "very soon" without saying when very soon was. He still insisted the United States would have to make an apology to Iran, but that the Carter Administration had already begun doing that "in practice." He suggested that a further step in that direction might be for the United States to fly away with the four communications surveillance planes it had given Saudi Arabia after the fighting broke out.

Washington said the planes would stay where they were, but repeated its long-standing willingness to unfreeze Iran's assets and expedite the embargoed $500 million shipment of military equipment Iran had ordered if the Americans came home. The president did endeavor to spread a little oil on troubled waters in oil-short Iran by remarking that that country had been a victim of "aggression" by "an invading nation."

As for Rajai's hot-cold statements, the White House said, "It is going to take us a little while to figure out the difference between the Rajai who spoke last night (at the U.N.) and the Rajai who spoke this morning (at the news conference)."

Who are the bad guys? An Iraqi soldier comforts a crying Iranian baby in his sister's arms. △

Air Raid. Iraqi soldiers man anti-aircraft positions on the roof of the national radio and television headquarters in Baghdad, waiting for continued strikes by Iranian planes. ▷

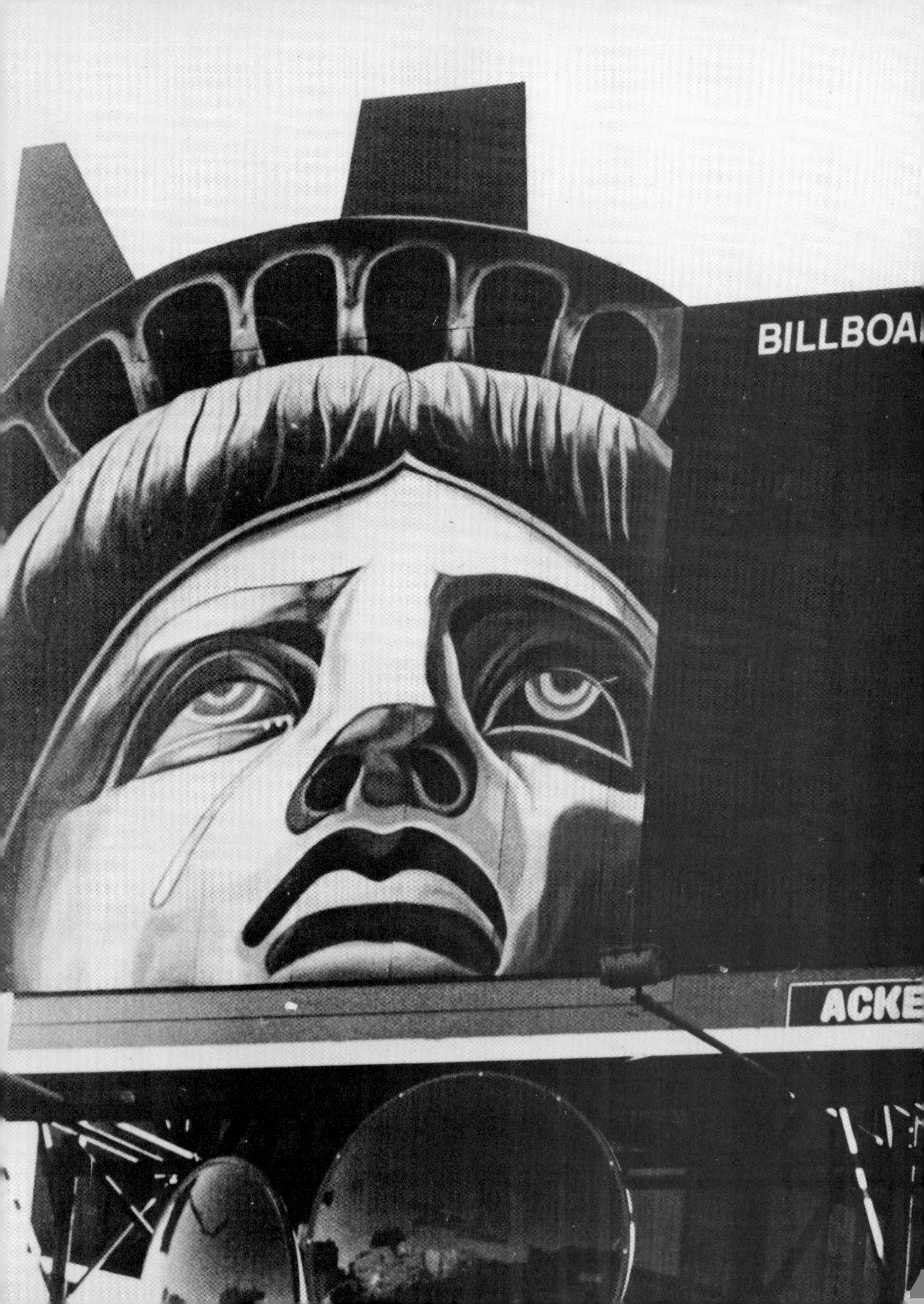
BILLBOA
ACKE

EDITORIAL

IRAN?

DAY

It had been exactly a year. A leap year. Five pounds of sugar, $1.30 then, were $2.60 now. The prime interest rate was going to 21 percent. Dr. Herman Tarnower, the diet doctor, was dead. Murdered. George Meany had died. And Tito. And Justice William O. Douglas. Richard Queen had a desk job at the State Department. It was election eve on . . .

DAY 366

As the campaign speaker, Jimmy Carter was like a sword swallower with a two-edged blade. One slip either way. . .

Obviously, the safe return of the hostages could turn a close election his way. A muff, or a reaction to unfulfilled hopes could as easily help Ronald Reagan.

"There was a time when the United States could determine who would be head of state in Iran," commented *Der Spiegel*, the West German weekly. "But in 1980, a fanatical ayatollah could decide the election of the U. S. president."

Carter had to walk presidentially yet chew gum at the same time, stand above partisanship yet be alert to the politics of the hostage crisis. At the same time, Reagan had to tiptoe around an emotion-laden issue. He did.

"All I can tell you is that I think this is too sensitive to make any comment at all," he told newsmen as he headed for church.

Nor did the Iranians seem oblivious to America's political drama. Reagan to them was a hard-liner, an unknown quantity.

"Reagan would be much worse than Carter," said Ali Reza Nobari, thirty-two-year-old head of the Iranian Central Bank. "I honestly believe that, more and more, the closer the election gets. Reagan is a danger to international peace."

As October waned, the Carter Administration lathered with soft soap, but gently. The president said at a campaign stop in Ohio that as soon as the hostages were freed, he would unfreeze the assets, stop the trade embargo which had blocked the arms deliveries and resume "normal commerce" with Iran. At the United Nations, Ambassador McHenry said: "The cohesion and stability of Iran is in the interest of the stability and prosperity of the region as a whole. The national integrity of Iran is today threatened by the Iraqi invasion."

But the president was cautious not to overdo it. "We have been disappointed too many times," he said. "So let's just hope and pray they come back—and not set a particular date on it."

But Carter the fisherman knew there were nibbles in Tehran. The Majlis was heading for a vote on the very eve of the American election. There was a "delicious shudder" of rumors, said John Trattner, State Department spokesman. Some diplomats there, however, thought Carter was lighting too many candles of hope, given the discords in Iran.

"We don't know what's happening, because the Iranians don't know what's happening," said one.

Bankers noted that it might be easy for Carter to say he would free Iran's money in the United States. What he had done with the pen, he could undo with the pen. But that would not sweep away all the liens, the questions of who would pay the interest and how much. Rearranging everything would be "like putting the omelet back into the egg," said one New York banker.

Nonetheless, as the rumors persisted, the president did not entirely stifle them. In West Germany phones were installed at the military hospital in Wiesbaden to handle the hostages' calls. Doctors were readied. Ambulance planes were on standby. Newsmen, those harbingers of a change in the weather, were flocking to Wiesbaden and Zurich, stops that Richard Queen had made upon his release.

As Americans prepared to vote, so, too, did the Majlis.

* * *

Hojatolislam Mohammed Moussavi Khoeini, a counselor to the militants and a member of the Majlis commission on the hostages that had finally been organized, said: "If the United States accepts our conditions, the hostages could be flown out of Iran by Monday (election eve)."

The commission was recommending adoption of the Ayatollah's four points. The debate began October 26, a Sunday, Day 358, in secret session. It was soon postponed to the next day. There was resistance in the assembly. Ayatollah Mohammed Beheshti, the leader of the hard-liners, said, "The United States has not accepted the Imam's conditions." Four days later, the hard-liners boycotted the session, preventing a quorum. Ayatollah Sadegh Khalkhali, the so-called "hanging judge" who had sent more than a hundred people to their executions, cursed the boycotters as "truant boys" and pounded his fists so furiously on a table that his turban fell off. The debate was put then off until Sunday, November 2, Day 365.

An uproar broke out when Khalkhali was accused of

Jimmy Carter campaigns in a cascade of balloons in Texarkana, Texas, while Reagan forces are wary of an "October surprise" to bring the hostages home on election eve.

proposing to trade the hostages for military equipment. Speaker Rafsanjani called a recess. On return, the delegates heard Khoeini read the commission's terms. They were the same as Khomeini's. The delegates voted. The proposals passed. But there was a string. The Majlis decided not to release the hostages as a body, but in groups as each of its terms were met. This was counter to U.S. insistence that they all be freed together. But now the ball was in President Carter's court.

•   •   •

The president was campaigning in Chicago when he was notified early Sunday morning. He cut short the final stops on his agenda and left at 5:23 A.M. for Washington on Air Force One. There he conferred with Brzezinski, Muskie, Harold Brown and Mondale.

Was the October "surprise" going to come in November, two days before the election? It was a thought one might be excused for savoring, if one had been a cautious fisherman. It was also possible the fish might wriggle away, raising questions of a fish story.

"The level of cynicism about the whole thing (among American voters) was high," said a Carter aide. "We had to play it absolutely straight. Being seen as too eager, conniving, or as the ayatollah's beneficiary were all highly dangerous."

The administration sent a careful response to Tehran via the Swiss Embassy there. "We basically said we would be willing to meet the conditions to the extent we can under our Constitution and laws," said an American official. Carter himself went on television for five minutes that Sunday night. He said the decision in the Majlis, as well as the agreement of the militants to turn responsibility for the hostages over to the government, were "a significant development." Carter vowed to protect the nation's honor and to bring the hostages home safely. He was mindful of the political implications.

"We are within two days of an important national election. Let me assure you that my decisions on this crucial matter will not be affected by the calendar." Then he got ready to fly to Seattle for a final campaign swing and then home to Plains, Georgia, to vote.

•   •   •

In Hermitage, Pennsylvania, the 366th American flag was unfurled to the wind. It was raised by Richard Hermening whose son, Kevin, had been a hostage for just a year.

•   •   •

"None of the Above" was one of the most popular candidates in the presidential election. It had often been a mean-spirited campaign, more one of staged media events than of political substance. Reagan may not have won the one debate he had with Carter, but he certainly did not lose. Pat Caddell, the president's pollster, had the two candidates neck and neck. After the debate in Cleveland, Caddell had Reagan four-and-a-half points ahead. Then they drew even again. But by the last weekend, Caddell had Carter a disastrous ten points behind.

On the flight back to Plains, Jody Powell drew the short straw. He was to tell the president. He downed a stiff drink, procrastinated, then sought out his boss who was having a double martini.

•   •   •

Reagan wound up his campaign in a shopping mall near San Diego. Some feminist hecklers were shouting "ERA! ERA!"

"Aw, shut up!" Reagan snapped. Then he chuckled. "My mother always told me that I should never say that. But this is my last night of a long campaign, and I thought just once I could say it."

•   •   •

Reagan, of course, won a landslide victory in the electoral college the next day, taking 483 votes to Carter's 49. His popular margin was as Caddell had forecast—ten points. The pollster thought that all the publicity given the possible return of the hostages that last weekend had been a critical factor. Much had been made of the president's competence or lack of it. Hopes had been raised high, but on Election Day, Day 367, the Americans were still prisoners.

The issue of the hostages had long been a wound for the administration. The weekend drama reminded voters that, after all, the president had been able to do nothing despite trying for a year and a day. That "ripped the scab off the wound," said a Carter aide.

President Carter campaigns through Manhattan while across the street, at the Chase Bank, Iranian accounts gather interest.

27

John Lennon was shot dead by a fan in New York. Russia was poised to invade Poland. President-elect Reagan picked former Watergate aide Alexander Haig as his Secretary of State. The Iranians set a rug merchant's fee of $24 billion for the hostages who were celebrating their second Christmas on . . .

DAY 418

Back in the bad old days, in fact back when George Washington was inaugurated as first president of the United States, twenty-one Americans captured by pirates were held hostage in Morocco.

The Moroccans wanted $41,000 for their release, $25,000 for the treaty doing so and $25,000 worth of naval stores—timber, cordage, pitch and the like—every year, indefinitely. The United States had no navy. Morocco was a long ways away. It paid.

More than one cent for tribute.

The day after Reagan's election, Rajai had said it would have no effect on the negotiations for the hostages' release. But the Iranians had a track record on Jimmy Carter. He had reached for the gun once, but the rest of the time he had spoken softly and not wielded a big stick. The Iranians had no way of knowing whether Reagan would be trigger happy. So a customer in the shop was better than two out in the street.

Furthermore, there was the war. It had not been the blitzkreig Iraq had hoped for. Khorramshahr had fallen, sort of, but Iranian irregulars were still shooting in the rubble. Abadan was a mess and traffic in Tehran had pulled over to the curb, gasless. But the Iranian armed forces had not collapsed. Quite the contrary. They had fought to a stalemate. It would be nice, however, to get all the spare parts that lay in storage at McGuire Air Force Base in New Jersey. Bani-Sadr said as much.

And an Iranian politician didn't need a masters degree in business from Stanford to know that Washington had no desire for a country rich in oil to collapse into the arms of Russia.

There was still a core of hard-liners in the Iranian government. Ghotbzadeh got his reward on November 7, Day 370, when he was thrown in jail for criticizing them. But cooler heads waited for the United States to respond to the terms of the Majlis. On November 10, Day 373, Warren Christopher delivered the American answer to the Algerian intermediaries in Algiers.

"It's up to the Iranians," said Carter. "I've had a timetable in mind for more than a year that has never been reached."

The sooner the better, said Bani-Sadr while visiting the front. "During a war, time is a decisive element."

• • •

There was some feeling matters were coming into the home stretch. News organizations were opening their checkbooks to the hostage relatives, offering to fly them to Wiesbaden in return for exclusives. In Homer, Illinois, Paul Lewis's mother, Gloria, quit her job as a school crossing guard to get away from reporters. Jerry Plotkin's wife, Deborah, wished aloud that *The New York Times* and *The Washington Post* would not always call her in Sherman Oaks, California, after midnight to get her reactions. "Anytime something exciting is happening in Iran they want my reaction. But I do not always have a reaction."

Allyssa Keough was ever willing to talk with newsmen. "I don't want people to forget. This is the only way I know how to help."

• • •

November 16, Day 379: Henry Kissinger says he expects the hostages will be released before Reagan is sworn in January 20, Day 444.

November 17, Day 380: Speaker Rafsanjani says the Majlis has spoken. The matter is now in the hands of the government.

November 20, Day 383: The United States has accepted Iran's terms "in principle," Muskie says. Details remain to be negotiated.

November 22, Day 385: Rajai says the American answer is "neither explicit nor clear." The United States will send another reply.

December 5, Day 398: The United States says further delay could jeopardize settlement of the crisis in early 1981. Iran denies a report the hostages have finally been turned over to the government. Khomeini has ordered Ghotbzadeh released from jail. The former foreign minister said it was the first time he had slept since the revolution.

December 11, Day 404: Iran says it won't accept a determination by U.S. courts as to who owns the Shah's money.

December 12, Day 405: Iran says the U.S. proposals are "more positive."

December 20, Day 413: Rajai said the Shah's wealth is the only remaining problem.

December 21, Day 414: Iran says the United States

Special Christmas. Apart from the others in the Foreign Ministry building, hostage Bruce Laingen, right, U.S. charge d'affairs, shares Christmas with Vatican envoy Annible Bugnini and Iranian Roman Catholic archbishop Youhannan Issayi. ▷

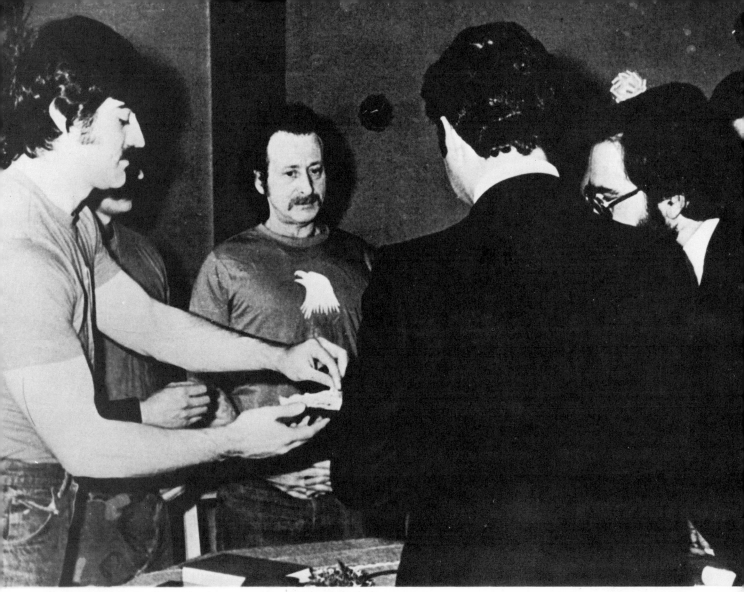

Holy Communion. Alan Golacinski takes communion while Jerry Plotkin looks on. ▲

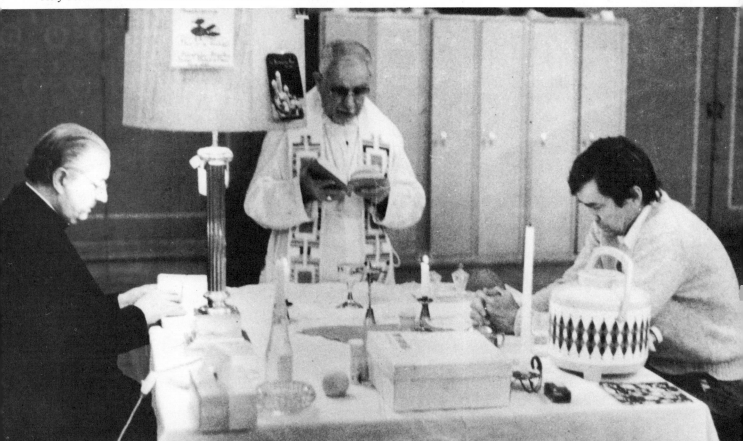

must deposit in Algiers $24 billion in cash and gold, its estimate of the Shah's funds and the frozen assets. Muskie says this is "unreasonable." Others say it is extortionate.

Not one cent for tribute.

*   *   *

For the second year, the national Christmas tree behind the White House was illuminated only by a single star at the top. The rest of the tree was kept dark as a "vigil of remembrance." It was lit fully for 417 seconds, the number of days of the hostages' captivity.

"Our American hostages have not yet come home," said Jimmy Carter. "But most of our prayers have been answered. They have stayed in touch with their families. So far as we know, they are safe, and their lives have been spared."

The problem of what the American response would be to an emperor's ransom and then some remained, however. For $24 billion Iran could buy twelve aircraft carriers. Dorothea Morefieled reminded a television reporter that, after all, the Iranians were rug merchants, hagglers. Almost of all of their spokesmen seemed more than willing to be rid of the crisis.

"God willing, we shall soon no longer have the hostage issue," said Rajai. The Americans could be home for Christmas or "the feast, or the birthday or whatever they call it."

Ayatollah Seyyed Beheshti, the clerical party leader, said, "The United States has to a large extent met our demands. There is now no basic catch in reaching a final solution."

Muskie said there was a catch. Iran was asking the United States to break American law to meet its demands.

Back to the drawing board.

*   *   *

This Christmas there were no American clergymen. But the Iranians allowed Monsignor Annibale Bugnini, the Vatican's envoy in Tehran, to hold Christmas Eve services. He was led blindfolded to what apparently was an apartment.

Behzad Nabavi, the head of Iran's commission on the hostages, said the prisoners were being held in hotels. At the same time, the United States said it believed some were in actual prisons. Nabavi said the hostages had been given ration cards, good for more than a year. "It will be no problem if they stay that long. We'll keep them if we have to for ten years."

The Iranians beamed film of Christmas greetings by the hostages to the United States. Thirty-four were shown in all, including for the first time, pictures of Ahern and Metrinko,

the accused CIA spies. The two women wore yellow ribbons in their hair, the American sign of remembrance.

Kathryn Koob asked her family back in Iowa to join as she sang "Away in a Manger." Her voice cracked as she sang. Her roomate, Elizabeth Ann Swift, said, "Tell everybody we're O.K."

"I'm feeling good, and I've lost weight for which I'm grateful," Koob said.

"God bless all of you, and God bless America," said Steve Lauterbach.

Joe Hall told his wife Cherilynn in Maryland: "I'm still

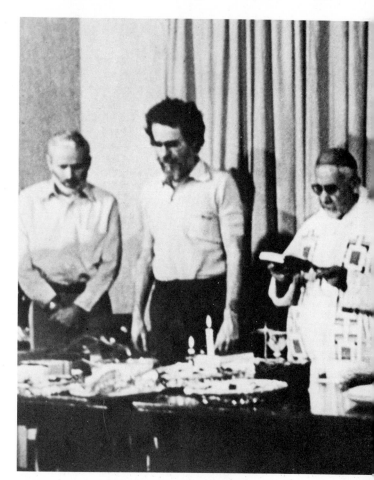

172

out here but I can hold on if you can, kid."

Phillip Ward reminded his son, Scott, not to forget to feed the birds during the winter.

John Miele had a beard. "Please don't worry. I'm alright. I get depressed at times, but I'm doing fine."

John McKeel's mother Wynona saw her son and got mad. "My blood started boiling when I started thinking that he was over there for Christmas and everyone else was here. And he never did anything."

"They're parading kidnap victims," said an indignant Barbara Rosen in Brooklyn. Speaking for FLAG, Louisa

Smiles on Christmas. Elizabeth Ann Swift of Washington, D.C., and Kathryn Koob of Jesup, Iowa.

Second Christmas in Captivity: Left to right, Thomas Schaefer, John Graves, Iranian Archbishop Youhannan Issayi, William Belk, Robert Ode, and Jerry Miele.

173

Kennedy asked: "Why are they doing this? Is it to soften us up so that we make demands on our government that we shouldn't?"

Ronald Reagan's comment was one Jimmy Carter might have often wanted to say but had diplomatically held his tongue. "Their captors are nothing better than criminals and kidnappers," he snapped.

Allyssa Keough worried that Reagan was planning to reach for the gun. "What this country needs is patience," she said.

So passed Day 418, and counting.

Latest demands: William Belk, Thomas Schaefer, Donald Hohman, and John Graves listen to the latest news on their release.

28

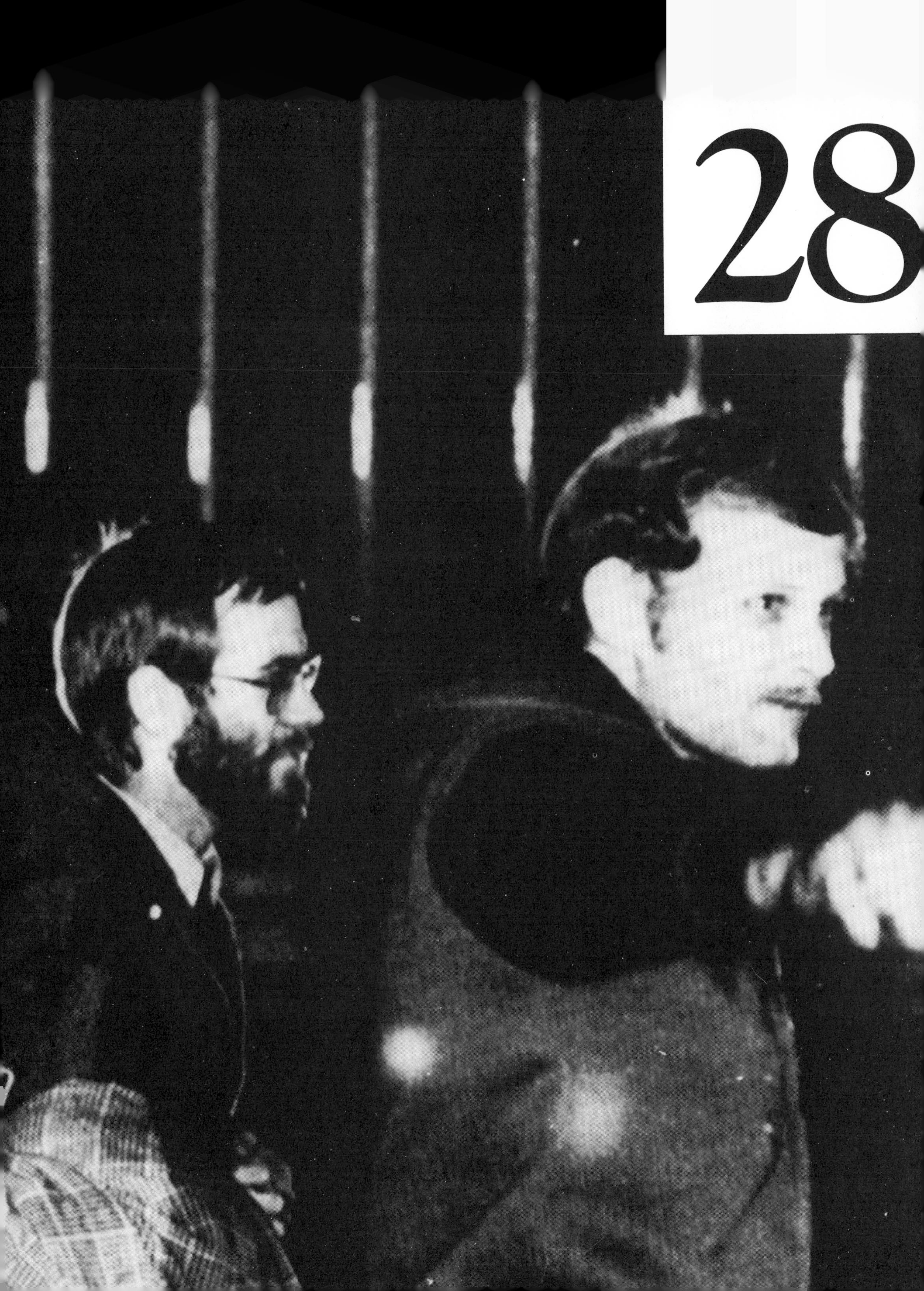

Time, for a change, was on the side of the hostages. Within minutes, actually, one Great Satan, Jimmy Carter, was about to be replaced by a possibly even Greater Satan, Ronald Reagan. The drama upstaged the former movie actor, beginning the first day of his presidency. There was a crueler calendar in Tehran.

DAY 444

In the end—and the end came at almost the very last second—it was a camel driver's bargain. They gave back what they took: people. We gave back money.

The Iranians kept turning the thumb screws until Carter and Reagan at the Capitol had already exchanged the office of president. The excruciating delays and haggling took place in a context of political confusion and intrigue in which the old term Byzantine might be updated with another—Iranian.

*   *   *

Whether as a ploy to speed the negotiations or as an expression of outrage many millions of Americans shared, Ronald Reagan said after Christmas: "I don't think you pay ransom for people that have been kidnapped by barbarians." Whether as a convenient way out or not, Tehran's many voices indicated they wanted to solve the impasse before Carter left office January 20. Carter set a deadline of January 16, Day 440. After that everything would have to start from scratch with the new administration.

Warren Christopher flew to Algiers. "This tragic event happened on our watch. We hope very much we can bring it to a successful conclusion on our watch," said the fifty-five-year-old diplomat-lawyer.

The government in Tehran said it now controlled the hostages, not the militants. Elizabeth Ann Swift had said on Christmas that they had been in a new location for a week. "It's lovely," she said. A British decorator thought the site was a hotel on the Caspian Sea that he had designed.

With the militants out of the picture, the hostages even more became the pawns of Iran's internal chess game. The fundamentalists controlled the Majlis and had increasingly isolated the moderate Bani-Sadr who preoccupied himself with fighting the war. What was said and done was as much for local political consumption as it was a message for Washington.

"Death to America," the Majlis delegates shouted in response to Reagan's likening them to barbarians. Behzad Nabavi, the thirty-eight-year-old Cabinet minister who was now chief negotiator for the hostages, was more soothing. "We don't take this very seriously. Reagan still thinks he is acting in Western movies and must behave in a wild manner."

Even Ayatollah Beheshti softened. "Anything acceptable to Algeria is acceptable to us." Ahmad Azizi of the hostage commission indicated Iran might settle for less than $24 billion. Both sides fingered their wallets—and the lapels of the three Algerian negotiators: Abdelkarim Gheraieb, ambassador to Iran; Rehda Malek, ambassador to the United States and Mohammed Seghier Mostefai, head of the national bank. There were hushed, hurried comings and goings of American bankers. Time, finally, was running down.

"The hostages are like a fruit from which all the juice has been squeezed out," said Nabavi. "Let us let them all go."

*   *   *

Announcement that the deal had been struck came January 18, Day 442. But two Algerian 727s were still on the ground in Tehran. "There's always that little voice that says, 'Careful, careful, careful,'" said Dorothea Morefield. "But it's getting awfully hard to listen to that voice. It's getting very, very faint."

"I feel like a scenic railroad going up and down," said John Smith of Rising Sun, Indiana, stepfather of hostage Donald Sharer. "We try not to get up, because these crazy people can do anything the last minute. But we can't help it. We're up."

Smith, of course, was right. On Monday, January 19, Day 443, Nabavi accused the private American banks of "subterfuge" in an appendix to the agreement Christopher had signed in Algiers the day before. The hostages had been examined by Algerian doctors, but the Boeings remained on the ground. Many believed the "rug merchants," the Moslem purists, the revolutionaries who had hounded the Shah to his grave, were stalling to torment James Earl Carter to the last minute of his presidency.

Which they were doing.

A woman returning from market stopped off at Barry Rosen's home in Brooklyn and talked to his father-in-law. She had seen the morning's headline "Coming Home" and on a hunch played the entries C-H in that day's Off-Track Betting daily double.

"So what comes in?" she said. "H-C, Home Coming."

"It paid $43, I think," said Rosen's father-in-law.

"What can you do?" the woman shrugged.

Flickering images. These brief glimpses from television by satellite.

*　　　*　　　*

Jimmy Carter, the 39th president, may have had similar thoughts at noon the next day as he heard the 40th president take the oath of office.

A newsman whispered a query if the hostages were airborne. Carter, now just a spectator, replied: "Don't know yet."

But even as he spoke, an Algerian jet with fifty-two Americans on board roared down the runway at Mehrabad Airport, drowning out onlookers' cries of "Death to America!" It lifted free and shot skyward, leaving the soil of Iran farther and farther behind until it had merged into the dark of a moonlit night.

It was five minutes before nine Iran time, the night of Day 444.

And no longer counting.

The national Christmas tree was redecorated and lit, all of it, all night. The torch of the Statue of Liberty was turned on in the middle of the day. Bells peeled across America and its people cheered, cried and felt, as much as 226 million people can, as one. The forest of flags in Hermitage, Pennsylvania, stood complete on January 21, 1981 . . .

179

DAY 1

...of the rest of their lives.

Two Iranian phantoms escorted the "Freedom Flight" to the country's borders, then U.S. fighters from Turkey took over. America had reclaimed her own.

The hostages, some of whom had not seen each other throughout their ordeal, "talked and talked and talked." Jimmy Lopez, it turned out, had been a Marine. It was he who had opened the door to let Lijek and the others out the back way of the consulate. He was urged to go with them. No, he said. It was his duty to stay with the embassy. Back in New York, Richard Queen, free to talk at last, told of mock midnight executions, the first crack of light he saw when moved from underground confinement in the Mushroom Inn, the chatter of birds, the distant laughter of school children.

As they boarded two buses at Rhein Main Air Base in Germany in a pre-dawn chill, some of the hostages dabbed at the misted windows with their fingers. They spelled for the world to see: "USMC" and "USA."

* * * *

Barry Rosen's mother, Sara, watched television with much of the rest of the nation far into the night. "He's free," she said, "and I'm free."

The whole country wore a yellow ribbon.

But there was a black arm band, too. For all the exultation and relief, it was not an entirely proud episode in American history. There had been a gentleman's agreement not to talk too much in public while lives were at stake. It had always been there during the campaign, an all but unspoken issue that may have been central to the unhorsing of a president. There had been no spy trials. The Iranians had haggled over American lives and ended up with what they had in the bank to begin with. New York's Mayor Ed Koch said the United States had paid ransom, in effect, but that was—would be— debatable. The Senate said it would hold hearings on how to prevent a recurrence. Undoubtedly questions would be asked, finally, as to why the embassy was left vulnerable in the first place despite its own warnings, why the Shah had been allowed to come, what Carter might have done and didn't.

"Until this country gets its pound of flesh, people will not be satisfied," said Clarence Ott, a logger in Snoqualmie, Washington.

That was an understandable reaction. So, too, was joy.

In Hermitage, 444 Stars and Stripes curled in the January wind, waving still over the land of the free.

180

Waving the flag: Thomas Schaefer waves a little American flag that says a lot. △

Terms of the Agreement:

—The United States pledges not to interfere in Iran's affairs.

—Iranian holdings of $1 billion in gold and $1.2 billion in cash and securities held by the U.S. Federal Reserve Bank is returned.

—Assets totalling more than $4 billion held by foreign branches of U.S. banks is returned.

—Of these monies, $3.6 billion will repay U.S. loans to Iran. Another $1.5 billion will be set aside to pay other bank loans.

—The estimated $3 billion of Iranian assets held by U.S. banks in domestic branches will be delivered to the Bank of England, half to be sent to Iran after six months, the rest to be put in a special fund to repay claims against that country. These claims will be decided by an international panel.

—The United States will freeze all property and assets of the Shah in the United States and help in an accounting.

—The United States will prohibit future law suits against Iran by Americans because of the hostage seizure or revolutionary action.

—The United States will end all trade sanctions and its claim before the World Court against Iran.

Thus, Iran got back less than half of the $8 billion to $10 billion of its assets.

The United States, said Walter Mondale, did not pay "a dime of American money" to get its hostages home.

Two roommates come home. Elizabeth Ann Swift (left) and Kathryn Koob wear smiles and yellow ribbons as they leave plane in Algiers. △

181

Cyrus Vance, now former Secretary of State, steps from the bus that carried him and the hostages from the airport to the Wiesbaden U.S. Air Force Hospital. ◁

Entrance to Rhein-Main Air Force Base AFB: Through these portals passed, after 444 days, the 52 Americans whose odyssey was finally over. ▷

Troubleshooter. Deputy Secretary of State Warren Christopher arrives in Algiers for hostage negotiations.

Jimmy Carter ends a frantic day in a post-midnight statement that release is at hand.

"He's coming, home, Freckles," Barbara Timm tells the family pet after the agreement is signed.

A beginning and an end: Carter watches his successor sworn in. A hostage was to say Carter had "rolled the dice" on letting the Shah into the United States and the 52 paid the price.

Unidentified bankers: Algiers becomes an international banking center as two more arrive for last-minute negotiations. ▽

183

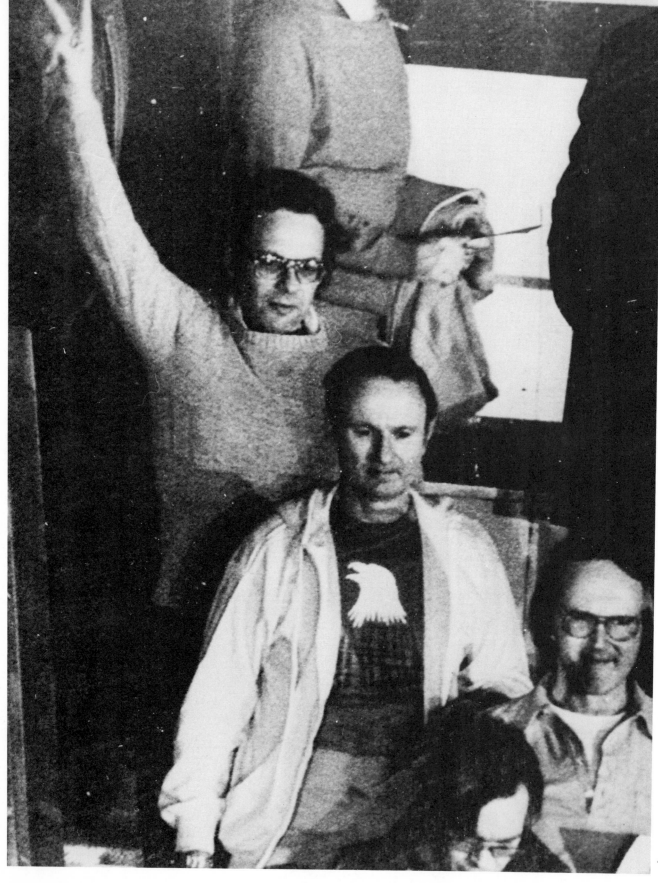

*Some came home with eagles flying. Donald Sharer flashes a victory sign
with fellow hostages.*

"W-a-r-r-e-n C-h-r-i-s-t-o-p-h-e-r," wrote the American diplomat, and penned an end to the crisis.

Hospital planes, called Nightingales, waited in Germany for the release, destination undetermined, condition of their future passengers unknown.

Tree-ribboning at Wiesbaden: Air Force wives at Wiesbaden tie yellow ribbons around young oak trees in welcoming preparations.

THE 52

Information on many of the hostages was sketchy throughout their imprisonment. An official list of names, addresses and ages was not issued. There were no official biographies.
Much of the information on the captives came from their families and friends.

THOMAS AHERN

Ahern was raised in Fond du Lac, Wisconsin, where his father, now dead, was a plumbing contractor. One of five children, he was an Eagle Scout, a member of the high school basketball team and played the piano. He is a 1954 graduate of Notre Dame University and served in the Army for three years before joining the foreign service. He was sent to Tehran in 1979 as a State Department attache and was the embassy's narcotics control officer. He is forty-eight years old, married to Gisela; they have a twelve-year-old daughter. They live in Falls Church, Virginia.

CLAIR CORTLANDT BARNES

Barnes is thirty-five years old, from Falls Church, Virginia.

WILLIAM BELK

A native of West Columbia, South Carolina, Belk grew up in Seattle, Washington, and served twenty-two years in the Air Force and the Marines before joining the State Department in 1974. He was communications and re-

cord officer at the embassy. He is forty-four years old, married; he and his wife, Angela, have two sons, Steven, aged twenty-two, and Allen, aged fourteen.

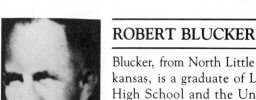

ROBERT BLUCKER

Blucker, from North Little Rock, Arkansas, is a graduate of Little Rock High School and the University of Wisconsin. He served in the Navy, then joined the State Department in 1958. He was an economics officer who specialized in oil matters. Blucker, aged fifty-three, is single.

DONALD COOKE

A native of Long Island, New York, Cooke (called "Donny" by his friends) grew up in Cleveland and lives in Memphis, Tennessee. He is twenty-five years old, holds a degree in geology from Ohio State University and has done graduate work in economics. Cooke joined the foreign service in November 1978. Cooke was sent to Tehran in July 1979 and served as vice consul at the embassy.

WILLIAM DAUGHERTY

About thirty-three years old, Daugherty attended Tulsa Central High School in 1963–65, then transferred to the Oklahoma Military Academy at Claremore. He attended Oklahoma State University, enlisted in the military and later went to work for the State Department. He is from Ossining, New York.

ROBERT ENGELMANN

A Navy lieutenant commander from Hurst, Texas, the thirty-three-year-old Engelmann was Navy attache at the embassy. When taken hostage, he had less than one week to serve in his tour of duty.

WILLIAM GALLEGOS

A Marine corporal who grew up in the Mexican–American neighborhood of Pueblo, Colorado. Gallegos, aged twenty-two, is the eldest of four children. A graduate of Pueblo East High School, Gallegos played football, was an expert in karate and liked outdoor sports. In 1977, a year after graduation, he joined the Marines and served a tour of duty in Okinawa. He was sent to Tehran in July 1979.

BRUCE GERMAN

The embassy budget officer, German is forty-three years old and lives in Rockville, Maryland. According to his wife, Marge, he arrived in Tehran about five weeks before the takeover.

DUANE GILLETTE

A graduate of Hempfield (Pennsylvania) High School, Gillette, aged twenty-four, lives in Columbia, Pennsylvania. He joined the Navy in 1975 and was assigned to Tehran in July 1979 as a communications specialist.

ALLAN GOLACINSKI

The eldest of four children, the twenty-nine-year-old Golacinski is a civilian who worked at the embassy as a security officer. His mother, Pearl, was one of several relatives of hostages who visited European leaders in efforts to free the captives. He is from Silver Springs, Maryland.

JOHN GRAVES

A former Detroit, Michigan, schoolteacher, the fifty-three-year-old Graves joined the State Department in 1963. He served in Vietnam and Africa, receiving a meritorious service award for duty in the Congo in 1964. In 1973, he was promoted to foreign service senior inspector. He and his wife, Bonnie, have six children.

JOSEPH HALL

A native of Oklahoma, Hall grew up in Bend, Oregon. Aged thirty-one, Hall joined the Army after graduation from Bend High School in 1967 and was stationed in Indonesia and Greece. Sent to Iran in August 1979, Hall served as a warrant officer. He is married to Cherlynn, and lives in Little Falls, Minnesota.

KEVIN HERMENING

At age twenty, Hermening was the youngest hostage. Assigned first to West Germany, he was ordered to serve in Iran at the last minute. A 1977 graduate of Oak Creek High School, Oak Creek, Wisconsin, he is the oldest of five children. His parents divorced when he was thirteen. His mother, Barbara, is married to Kenneth Timm. Mrs. Timm visited Iran in 1980 in an unsuccessful attempt to win the release of her son.

187

DONALD R. HOHMAN

A Marine Corps medic, Hohman has been in the service for six years. He attended James Marshall High School in Sacramento, California, and lived in West Sacramento. He was transferred from Germany to the embassy in Tehran in August 1979. His wife and their two sons remained in West Germany. He is thirty-nine.

LELAND HOLLAND

Holland, aged fifty-three, is a native of Scales Mound, Illinois, and lives in Fairfax, Virginia. An Army colonel and a veteran of Vietnam, Holland arrived in Iran in August 1979 for what was to be a three-year tour. He served as chief of security at the embassy in Tehran. He is the eldest of three children and is married with six children.

MICHAEL HOWLAND

Howland, aged thirty-four, of Alexandria, Virginia, was one of the three hostages taken at the foreign ministry, rather than at the embassy.

CHARLES A. JONES JR.

A native of Memphis, Tennessee, Jones joined the Air Force after graduation from high school. After his discharge in 1962, he worked as an apprentice draftsman, and later joined the foreign service. He served in Egypt, West Germany, the Congo, Israel and France. Jones was a teletype operator for International Communications Agency. He is forty years old, married and has four children. He was the only black hostage among the remaining fifty-two.

MALCOLM KALP

Kalp was accused by the militants of being a CIA agent, based on documents they released. He is forty-two years old, and from Fairfax, Virginia.

MOORHEAD KENNEDY JR.

A Harvard Law School graduate, Kennedy, of Washington, D.C., is an Islamic law scholar and economics expert. He went to Iran in September 1979 as an economic specialist for the State Department. He is fifty years old, married and has four children. His wife, Louisa, the spokeswoman for FLAG (Family Liaison Action Group) led relatives of several hostages on a European mission.

WILLIAM F. KEOUGH JR.

Keough, aged fifty, is from Waltham, Massachusetts. He is a graduate of Boston College and Boston University and is a long-time educator. He was principal of the American School in Tehran, a private institution which closed after the fall of the Shah. He had returned to Iran on November 1, 1979, to collect school records and was staying at the embassy when it was seized. He often drew stares in Tehran because of his size—six feet six inches tall and more than 300 pounds.

STEVE KIRTLEY

A Marine corporal from Little Rock, Arkansas, Kirtley was an embassy security guard. He had dropped out of McClellan High School in Little Rock and had written to school officials to ask how he could get his degree; he said he wanted to go to college after getting out of the Marines. Aged twenty-two, Kirtley comes from a military family—his father is a disabled World War II veteran and two brothers and a sister are in the service.

KATHRYN KOOB

Koob, one of six daughters of Harold and Elsie Koob, grew up on a small farm in Iowa and went to Wartburg College, a Lutheran school in Waverly, Iowa. She worked for the church for several years, then became a teacher. She joined the foreign service in June 1969 and served in Africa and Romania. Koob, aged forty-three, was an International Communications Agency officer and director of the Iran-American Society in Tehran.

FREDERICK LEE KUPKE

Kupke, known as "Rick," is part Kiowa Indian. He spent part of his childhood in the Meers area of southwestern Oklahoma and attended a Commanche County elementary school. He attended Cameron University in Lawton, Oklahoma, before joining the State Department. He served in the communication section of the foreign service in the Sinai and volunteered for duty in Iran. Kupke was scheduled to leave Tehran November 5—the day after the embassy was seized. He is thirty-four years old and lives in Francesville, Indiana.

BRUCE L. LAINGEN

Laingen, aged fifty-seven, one of the three hostages seized at the foreign ministry, was the charge d'affaires, the highest ranking U.S. diplomat in Iran at the time the embassy was seized. Laingen is a thirty-year foreign service veteran. He served as U.S. ambassador to Malta and deputy assistant secretary

of state for European affairs. He and his wife, Penne, have three sons and live in Bethesda, Maryland.

STEVE LAUTERBACH

A graduate of Chaminade High School in Dayton, Ohio, Lauterbach received a bachelor's degree from Bowling Green State University and a master's degree from the University of Michigan. He worked in a library in Fresno, California, before joining the foreign service. Lauterbach, aged twenty-nine, began working in Washington, D.C. in June 1978. In March 1979, he was sent to Iran to obtain personal items of Americans who had been evacuated earlier.

GARY LEE

Lee, from Falls Church, Virginia, worked as a business administrator at the embassy for four years. He previously served as consular officer in Bombay. He is married and has a daughter. He celebrated his thirty-seventh birthday in captivity.

PAUL LEWIS

A Marine sergeant who served in the embassy security guard force, Lewis, aged twenty-three, arrived in Tehran only one day before the takeover. He graduated in 1975 from Homer (Illinois) High School, where he was on the football team and was homecoming king. He enlisted in the Marines in 1977 and served in Budapest before his transfer to Iran.

JOHN W. LIMBERT JR.

A thirty-seven-year-old State Department political officer, Limbert is from Washington, D.C. He is married and has a son and a daughter.

JAMES MICHAEL LOPEZ

A 1976 graduate of Globe High School, Globe, Arizona, the twenty-two-year-old Lopez attended Mesa Community College for half a year. He then enlisted in the Marines where he rose to sergeant.

JOHNNY McKEEL JR.

A Marine sergeant from Balch Springs, Texas, McKeel attended high school in the Dallas suburb of Mesquite. In the summer of 1979, the twenty-seven-year-old signed up for his second tour of duty with the Marines and asked to be sent to a special school for foreign embassy guards.

MICHAEL J. METRINKO

A thirty-four-year-old bachelor, Metrinko was born in Olyphant, Pennsylvania, and graduated from Georgetown University. He went to the Middle East first as a Peace Corps volunteer, working in Turkey and Iran. He later joined the State Department and was assigned to Syria, Greece and Iran, where he was consul in Tabriz.

JERRY MIELE

Miele, single, graduated form Hurst High School in Mount Pleasant, Pennsylvania. He served in the U.S. Navy and joined the State Department in 1962. He was assigned to the embassy in Tehran in March 1979. He is forty-two years old.

MICHAEL MOELLER

A Marine staff sergeant from Loup City, Nebraska, Moeller is a nine-year veteran of the service. Moeller served for two years at the U.S. embassy in Islamabad, Pakistan before his transfer to the embassy security guard in Tehran in July 1979. He is twenty-nine years old and married with two children.

BERT MOORE

Moore, an administration counselor at the embassy, was assigned to Tehran in July 1979 after serving in Africa, France and Canada. He is forty-five years old. He and his wife, Marjorie, have four children. He is from Mount Vernon, Ohio.

RICHARD MOREFIELD

A native of San Diego, California, Morefield has a bachelor's degree from the University of San Francisco and a master's degree from the University of California. He joined the State Department in 1953 after serving two years in the Army and was appointed consul-general in Tehran in the summer of 1979. He is fifty-one years old. He and his wife, Dorothea, have two sons.

PAUL NEEDHAM

An Air Force captain from Bellevue, Nebraska, Needham was assigned to the Air Force Logistic Command at Wright Patterson Air Force Base in Ohio. He was in Iran on temporary assignment to assist the Iranians with repairs and maintenance of American-supplied aircraft. Needham, aged thirty, is divorced.

ROBERT C. ODE

A retired diplomat who was on temporary duty at the embassy, the sixty-four-year-old Ode is believed to be the oldest of the hostages. Ode went to Tehran on October 3, 1979, for what was to have been a forty-five-day tour of duty. He is from Sun City West, Arizona, and is married.

GREGORY A. PERSINGER

A Marine sergeant from Seaford, Delaware, Persinger was serving his second tour of duty in Iran. He had volunteered to stay on as an embassy guard after the Shah was overthrown. He observed his twenty-third birthday on Christmas Day 1980.

JERRY PLOTKIN

Plotkin, a businessman on his first trip outside the U.S. happened to be visiting the embassy at the time of the takeover. A former household goods salesman, he is forty-seven years old, married to Deborah. He is from Sherman Oaks, California.

REGIS RAGAN

An Army master sergeant, Ragan served in Germany and Vietnam, where he was decorated with the Bronze Star and several other awards. He was assigned as an embassy guard in Tehran in 1974. Thirty-eight-year-old Ragan is from Johnstown, Pennsylvania.

DAVID ROEDER

An Air Force lieutenant colonel, Roeder grew up in Whitefish Bay, Wisconsin, a Milwaukee suburb, where his father was assistant high school principal. Roeder, an Eagle Scout, played football in high school and was in the ROTC. He joined the Air Force after graduation from college and flew more than one hundred combat missions in Vietnam. He was the deputy Air Force attache in Tehran and had arrived only three days before the embassy was seized. He is thirty-eight years old. He and his wife, Susie, have two children.

BARRY ROSEN

Rosen, from Brooklyn, New York, was the press attache at the embassy. He is thirty-five years old and has two children. His wife, Barbara, was among a group of relatives of the hostages who visited European leaders to seek their help.

WILLIAM B. ROYER JR.

Royer, a forty-nine-year-old school-teacher, has worked in the Middle East since 1963. He was working at the Iranian-American Society in Tehran when he and another American were seized and taken to the embassy. He is from West University Place, Texas, a suburb of Houston and is a University of Texas graduate.

THOMAS SCHAEFER

An Air Force colonel, Schaefer has been in the military for almost thirty years. In 1978, he was assigned to a three-year tour in Iran and served as a military defense attache at the embassy. In April 1980, while in captivity,

191

he was named head of the Air Force ROTC program at the University of Washington; the appointment was to be effective in August. Aged fifty, he is from Tacoma, Washington. He and his wife, Betty, have one son.

CHARLES SCOTT

A lieutenant colonel in the Army, Scott was assigned to the embassy in 1979. It was his second tour of duty in Iran; he served there as an Army attache before being sent to Vietnam. He is forty-eight years old, from Stone Mountain, Georgia; married with two children.

DONALD A. SHARER

A State Department employee, Sharer was formerly based at the Naval Air Station at Virginia Beach, Virginia. His family lives in Chesapeake, Virginia.

RODNEY V. SICKMANN

A sergeant, Sickmann ("Rocky") enlisted in the Marines at the end of his senior year in high school. He was assigned to Tehran in October 1979. He is twenty-three years old and grew up in Krakow, Missouri, a farming hamlet fifty miles west of St. Louis.

JOSEPH SUBIC JR.

Subic, aged twenty-three, is from Redford Township, Michigan. At the age of seventeen he left Bowling Green (Ohio) High School to join the Army and rose to staff sergeant.

ELIZABETH ANN SWIFT

Swift, aged thirty-nine, from Washington, D.C., was the second-ranking political officer at the embassy.

VICTOR TOMSETH

One of the three hostages originally held at the foreign ministry in Tehran rather than in the embassy, Tomseth is a 1959 graduate of Springfield (Oregon) High School and a 1963 graduate of the University of Oregon. He joined the foreign service in 1967 after a stint in the Peace Corps and went to Iran in 1976. He is thirty-nine years old, married with two children. He lives in McLean, Virginia.

PHILIP R. WARD

Ward, aged thirty, lives in Culpeper, Virginia. He and his wife, Connie, have one son, Scott.